Teresa Wall.

EXPERIENCE
CONTRADICTION
NARRATIVE
&
IMAGINATION

EXPERIENCE, CONTRADICTION, NARRATIVE & IMAGINATION:

Selected papers
of
David Epston & Michael White
1989-1991

Dulwich Centre Publications
South Australia

David Epston	Michael White
The Family Therapy Centre	Dulwich Centre
6 Goring Road	345 Carrington Street
Sandringham, Auckland 4	Adelaide 5000
New Zealand	South Australia
ph: 64 - 9 - 846 6306	ph: 61 - 8 - 223 3966

Copyright © 1992 by Dulwich Centre Publications

ISBN 0 646 09455 6

published by:
Dulwich Centre Publications
Hutt Street PO Box 7192
Adelaide South Australia 5000
ph: 61 - 8 - 223 3966

No part of this book may be reproduced or transmitted by any process whatsoever without the prior written permission of the Publisher.

Printed and Manufactured in Australia
by Graphic Services Pty Ltd, Northfield, South Australia

ACKNOWLEDGEMENTS

We would like to thank Ann Epston and Cheryl White for their encouragement of, and support for, our work over the years. Without this, much of what is written here would not be.

Special thanks is due to Jane Hales for her work in organizing this material into book form.

CONTENTS

INTRODUCTION: 7

CHAPTER I:
Consulting Your Consultants: The documentation of 11
alternative knowledges - *David Epston & Michael White*

CHAPTER II:
A Conversation about AIDS and Dying 27
with *Michael White & David Epston*

CHAPTER III:
Temper Tantrum Parties: Saving face, losing face, 37
or going off your face! - *David Epston*

CHAPTER IV:
Family Therapy Training and Supervision in a World 75
of Experience and Narrative - *Michael White*

CHAPTER V:
A Problem of Belonging - *Jeremy & David Epston* 97

CHAPTER VI:
Self-Specialization - *Bryce Wilson & David Epston* 105

CHAPTER VII:
   Deconstruction and Therapy - *Michael White*   109

CHAPTER VIII:
   Strange and Novel Ways of Addressing Guilt   153
   - *David Epston*

CHAPTER IX:
   "I am a Bear": Discovering discoveries - *David Epston*   173

CHAPTER X:
   An Approach to Childhood Stealing with Evaluation   189
   of 45 Cases - *Fred W. Seymour & David Epston*

INTRODUCTION

This volume is a collection of papers that were published between 1989 and 1991, although some of them describe work that was developed at an earlier date. Our purpose in making these papers available in one source book is so that they can be read together. The papers cover a range of subjects including: personal reminiscence; particular therapeutic practices; practical approaches to various problems; theoretical, political and philosophical considerations; structures and issues pertaining to training and supervision; processes of questioning in the co-authorship of preferred stories, and so on.

Although our respective contributions are distinct, as is our style of writing, we acknowledge the extent to which we have shared ideas with each other, and worked together over the history of our friendship. Our colleagueship has consistently been extended through this interaction, despite the fact that the cities in which we live are geographically distant. And the enthusiasm that we have experienced for each other's work has been instrumental in the further exploration of those ideas and practices that were detailed in **Literate Means to Therapeutic Ends/Narrative Means to Therapeutic Ends**.

In our attempts to reflect, in a more specific sense, on this collection of papers and, in so doing, provide an overview for readers, we struggled with the same questions that many others have struggled with: How best to classify this work? Are there some relatively simple descriptive statements that might reasonably characterize it? So far, at least, our work seems to have defied any consistent classification. Although others have presented us with many simple and apparently conclusive descriptions of it, most of these descriptions have been widely disparate, and none of them have been wholly satisfying to us.

At times we have tried to respond to questions, from others, like the following:
- *"How might I describe your approach? Would it be appropriate to consider you to be brief, solution focused, or narrative therapists?"*
- *"The tradition of thought that you situate your work in is clearly non-foundationalist. But how might it be described in a more positive sense? For example, does it reflect a second-order cybernetic tradition, or does it reflect a constructivist tradition?"*
- *"Of all of those theories to which you refer, which have been the most significant in the development of this work? Would it be literary theory, critical theory, social theory, or something else?"*
- *"What are the contexts that you consider most relevant to your work? Do you privilege macro-contexts and emphasize matters of social organization, or do you privilege micro-contexts and emphasize notions of personhood and experience?"*
- *"What disciplines have been most relevant to the development of your work? Do you borrow more from anthropology, sociology, or philosophy?"*

Reviewing these and many other questions and, as well, our attempts to make an adequate response to them, provides some reassurance to us that our work defies any attempts at relatively simple totalizations of it. Reassurance, because any successful totalization of our work could run the risk of capturing and restricting us and our readers as well.

We have been steadfast in our refusal to name our work in any consistent manner. We do not identify with any particular "school" of family therapy, and are strongly opposed to the idea of our own contribution being named as a school. We believe that such a naming would only subtract from our freedom to further explore various ideas and practices, and that it would make it difficult for others to recognize their own unique contributions to developments in this work, which we regard to be an "open book".

There is another reason to resist such naming. With regard to ideas and practices, we do not believe that we are in any one place at a particular point in time, and rarely in particular places for very long. In making this observation, we are not suggesting that the developments in our work are sharply discontinuous - they are not. Nor are we suggesting that our values and our commitments are varying - they are not. And we are definitely not arguing for forms of eclecticism - which we eschew. However, we are drawing attention to the fact that one of the aspects associated with this work that is of central importance to us is the spirit of adventure. We aim to preserve this spirit, and know that if we accomplish this our work will continue to evolve in ways that are enriching to our lives, and to the lives of those persons who seek our help.

What will be the direction of this evolution? It could be tempting to make pronouncements about this. But these would be too hard to live by. And besides, our sense is that most of the "discoveries" that have played a significant part in the development of our practices, as described in this collection, have been made after the fact (in response to unique outcomes in our work with families), with theoretical considerations assisting us to explore and to extend the limits of these practices. We acknowledge the fact that it is always so much easier to be "wise" in hindsight than in foresight.

These comments represent our way of introducing readers to the many and varied ideas and practices described in this particular collection. We hope that you will then join us in adventure.

Michael White &
David Epston

CHAPTER I

CONSULTING YOUR CONSULTANTS:
The documentation of alternative knowledges

David Epston & Michael White

*Previously published in
Dulwich Centre Newsletter
1990, No.4.*

This is a revised version of a presentation given by the authors at the Australian Family Therapy Conference, Melbourne, 1985. Some notes relating to this presentation were originally published in the conference proceedings (White & Epston 1985).

In this paper we describe a therapeutic practice that encourages persons to document the solution knowledges, and the alternative knowledges about their lives and relationships, that have been resurrected and/or generated in therapy. These knowledges then become more available for persons to redeploy when necessary and for others to consult.

The "rite-of-passage" analogy provides a frame for this work. This analogy contributes to its conceptualization and organization. A protocol will be outlined for establishing persons as consultants to themselves and to others. As well, we will present and categorize an array of questions which assist persons to engage in an archaeology of their alternative knowledges.

RITE OF PASSAGE

We believe that the class of ritual referred to by van Gennep (1960) as a "rite of passage" has a great deal to offer as a metaphor for the process of therapy. van Gennep asserted that the rite of passage is a universal phenomenon for facilitating transitions, in social life, from one status and/or identity to another. He proposed a processual model of this rite, consisting of the stages of separation, liminality and reincorporation. In traditional cultures, the initiation of these stages is marked by ceremony.

At the separation stage, persons are detached from familiar roles/statuses and locations and enter an unfamiliar social world in which most of the taken-for-granted ways of going about life are suspended - a liminal space. This liminal space, which constitutes the second stage of a rite of passage, is "betwixt and between" known worlds and is characterized by experiences of disorganization and confusion, by a spirit of exploration, and by a heightened sense of possibility.

The third stage of reincorporation brings closure to the ritual passage and assists persons to relocate themselves in the social order of their familiar world, but at a different position. This different position is characteristically accompanied by new roles, responsibilities and freedoms. Traditionally, the arrival at this point is augmented by claims and declarations that the person has successfully negotiated a transition, and this is legitimated by communal acknowledgement.

Rite of Passage and Therapy

We have found that this rite of passage metaphor provides a useful map for orienting therapists to the process of therapy, and for assisting those persons who seek therapy in transiting from problematic statuses to unproblematic statuses (Epston 1985, 1987).

Our interpretation of this metaphor structures a therapy that encourages persons to negotiate the passage from novice to veteran, from client to consultant. Rather than instituting a dependency upon "expert knowledges", this therapy enables persons to arrive at a point where they can take recourse to certain alternative and "special" knowledges that they have resurrected and/or generated during the therapy.

In therapy, the "separation" stage can be invoked through a range of interventions, including those that encourage persons to distinguish themselves from their problems by engaging in externalizing discourses in relation to these problems (White 1989). This dislodges persons from certain familiar and taken-for-granted notions about problems and from the dominant internalizing discourses that guide their lives. This initiates the experience of liminality.

It is in this liminal space that new possibilities emerge which can be explored, and that alternative knowledges can be resurrected and/or generated. It is in this liminal space that persons' worlds are subjunctivized. When referring to the liminal phase of a rite of passage, Turner (1986) says:

I sometimes talk about the liminal phase being dominantly in the subjunctive mood of culture, the mood of maybe, might be, as if, hypothesis, fantasy, conjecture, desire - depending on which of the trinity of cognition, affect, and conation is situationally dominant. (p.42)

We believe that therapists can best gauge the extent of their participation in the liminal stage by the degree to which they lose track of time and are unable to estimate the length of the session, and by the degree to which they experience a sense of "communitas" with the persons who seek therapy. This sense of communitas is portrayed well by Turner (1967):

This liminal group is a community or community of comrades and not a structure of hierarchically arrayed positions. This comradeship transcends distinctions of rank, age, kinship position, and, in some kinds of cultic group, even of sex. (p.100)

The final stage of reincorporation brings the therapy to its conclusion. It is through reincorporation that the alternative knowledges that have been resurrected and/or generated become authenticated. It is through reincorporation that the new possibilities can be realized.

THE "TERMINATION AS LOSS" METAPHOR

We believe that, in the transformative process called therapy, what we would refer to as the reincorporation stage has been the least satisfactorily attended to aspect. It is our speculation that this has to do with the fact that the "termination-as-loss" metaphor has dominated the literature on this stage of therapy.

The dominance of the termination-as-loss metaphor is premised on a particular orientation to therapy. This is an orientation that privileges the therapeutic micro-world above all others.[1] It represents the final stage of therapy as one that is dominated by the loss of this micro-world and its central and supposedly all-important relationship, and by the requirement for an adjustment to "going it on your own".

We believe that this orientation to therapy - one that constructs an entirely separate and private stage for persons' lives - is in turn premised on certain cultural conceptions and practices. These include the dominant individualizing conception of personhood in Western culture, the essentialist notion of the self, the idea that the person is the source of all meaning, and the modern practices of the objectification of persons and their bodies which are common to the "disciplines" (Foucault 1973).

About the cultural specificity of this individualizing conception of personhood, Geertz (1976) has this to say:

The Western conception of the person as a bounded, unique cognitive universe, a dynamic centre of awareness, emotion, judgement and action organized into a distinctive whole is, however incorrigible it may seem to us, a rather peculiar idea within the concept of the world's cultures. (p.225)

We would refer to those therapies that are informed by these cultural conceptions and practices as the "therapies of isolation".

THE "REINCORPORATION" METAPHOR

In contrast to the practices informed by the termination-as-loss metaphor, the reincorporation metaphor would represent the final stage of therapy as one that centres around a rejoining of the person with others in a familiar social world, and would encourage the recruitment of others in the celebration and acknowledgement of the person's arrival at a preferred destination or status in life. We would refer to those therapies that are informed by these practices as the "therapies of inclusion".[2]

However, despite the possibilities that accompany the reincorporation metaphor, there have been some obstacles to the therapeutic practices that are suggested by it. For example, Kobak and Waters (1984), who have also referred to the rite of passage metaphor, draw attention to the practical difficulties in linking the micro-world of therapy to the world at large:

However, in relation to his [sic] more 'primitive' [sic] tribal counterpart, who manages a publicly recognized rite of passage, the family therapist is at a relative disadvantage in creating long-lasting, second-order change. The most apparent disadvantage is that the family therapist does not have the ties to the family's community and community norms that reinforce the changes that occur during the rite of passage once the participants return to ordinary life ... Such participation of the community in the change process serves to stabilize second-order changes that occur during the liminal rites. By operating without knowledge of community norms, the family therapist may create liminal change that is not sustained in the reaggregation phase.[3]
A developmental view of family problems may assist the therapist, yet the relative isolation of the therapist from the family's community remains a problem. Potential solutions to this dilemma have emerged in the form of involving the family 'network' or, less extensively, by activating the family kin system. The rite of passage analogy suggests that efforts should be further explored. (p.99)

For a number of years we have been experimenting, in various ways, to overcome the sort of obstacles referred to above. The feedback that we have received in response to this experimentation has convinced us of:
(a) the pertinence of the rite of passage metaphor and the appropriateness of considering the concluding stage of therapy as reincorporation, and
(b) the inappropriateness of a strong emphasis on the termination-as-loss metaphor for this stage of therapy.

Because it has been our preference to construe the concluding stage of therapy as reincorporation, this has given us cause for celebration with the persons who have sought therapy, rather than for commiseration. We have been able to challenge the conception of therapy as an exclusive and esoteric social space or individual stage, necessarily bound by rigid rules of privacy and exclusion.

We have assisted persons to explore various ways and means by which to counter the practices informed by this conception - to protest the limitations of this privacy. We have participated with persons in the publicizing and circulation of the alternative and preferred knowledges that have been resurrected and/or generated in therapy. We have joined with persons in their attempts to identify and recruit audiences to the performance of these alternative knowledges. And we have worked with persons in their efforts to document these knowledges in popular discourses and forms.

On reviewing our exploration of practices of reincorporation, we have classified various approaches that persons have found helpful. All of these approaches include the identification and recruitment of audiences for the authentication of change, and for the legitimation of alternative knowledges. The approaches include:
1. Celebrations, prize-givings and awards, attended by significant persons, including those who may not have attended therapy (White 1986);
2. Purposeful "news releases" whereby pertinent information as to the person's arrival at a new status is made available to various significant persons and agencies;
3. Personal declations and letters of reference, and
4. Consulting persons, in a formal sense, in relation to the solution knowledges that have enabled them to free their lives, and in relation to the alternative and preferred knowledges about their lives and relationships.

We addressed the first three approaches mentioned here in **Literate Means to Therapeutic Ends** (White & Epston 1989). In this paper we will restrict our discussion to the fourth of these approaches, presenting a protocol for what we refer to as "consulting your consultants".

CONSULTING YOUR CONSULTANTS

When persons are established as consultants to themselves, to others, and to the therapist, they experience themselves as more of an authority on their own lives, their problems, and the solution to these problems. This authority takes the form of a kind of knowledge and expertise which is recorded in a popular medium so that it is accessible to the consultant, therapist and potential others.

Throughout, the relative inequality of "therapist as helper" and "client as helped" is redressed. The gift of therapy is balanced by the gift of consultancy. We consider this reciprocity to be of vital importance in reducing the risk of indebtedness and replacing it by a sense of fair exchange. In **The Gift**, Mauss (1954) eloquently draws attention to the hazards inherent in such inequality:

To accept without returning or repaying more is to face subordination, to become a client and subservient ... to receive something is dangerous not only because it is illicit to do so, but also because it comes morally, physically, and spiritually from a person.

Protocol

Therapy is concluded with an invitation to persons to attend a special meeting with the therapist so that the knowledges that have been resurrected and/or generated in therapy can be documented. These knowledges will include those alternative and preferred knowledges about self, others and relationships, and those knowledges of problem-solving that have enabled persons to liberate their lives.

Persons are told that special attention will be given to an exploration of how they arrived at these knowledges, and of how they "made these knowledges work" for them. This gives persons advanced notice that they will be invited to provide some historical account of the struggle with their problems and of the discoveries that made it possible for them to free their lives. This serves to emphasize that these knowledges are significant, and that preservation of them through documentation is warranted.

Various means can be used for the purpose of substantiating and documenting these knowledges. Persons can choose from a variety of formats, including videotaping, audiotaping, autobiographical accounts, diaries, interview transcripts, etc.

If persons are concerned that they might have difficulty recalling relevant details, a sample of orienting questions can be supplied beforehand for them to reflect upon. This usually assists persons in preparation for the "consulting your consultants" interview.

Upon convening the meeting, the therapist runs through a prologue that further orients persons to its purpose. During this prologue future audiences are presupposed and explicitly referred to. The therapist then asks persons to give an account of their transition from a problematic status to a resolved one, and asks questions that encourage them to locate the significant events and steps in time in a sequential fashion. Alternatively, the therapist can provide her or his account of this transition, and invite persons to comment on it, elaborate upon it, make alterations to it, and to contribute their reflections in ways that dramatically bring this account to life.

By way of example, in the following text we present a small sample of the sort of questions that have been helpful in encouraging persons to articulate these knowledges. Readers will note that these questions are constructed in a grammar of agency, rather than of passivity and determinism. In responding to these questions, persons achieve a sense of personal agency. This is the experience of being able to play an active role in the shaping of one's own life, of possessing the capacity to influence developments in one's life to the extent of bringing about preferred outcomes.

Encouraging persons to respond to questions in a grammar of agency - or, as Douglas (1982) might put it, in the "active voice" - effectively counters their tendency of solely imputing the therapist's actions as critical to the emergence of solutions, and is essential to the constitution of self-knowledge. To quote from Harre (1983):

Self-knowledge requires the identification of agentive and knowing selves as acting within hierarchies of reasons. It follows that this kind of self-knowledge is, or at least makes available the possibility of, autobiography. (p.260)

We have grouped the questions according to several categories. Most of these categories have been discussed elsewhere (e.g. White 1988a), and they are offered to readers as an aid to the organization of this work. They should not be limiting to the reader's imagination, nor should they interfere with the expression of the reader's experience. Due to space considerations, these questions appear here in their more complex form. However, they can be easily modified according to the background and age of the persons seeking therapy.

Orientation Questions

These questions orient persons to the "consulting your consultants" interview, calling attention to the importance of:
- rendering a person's steps in the development of solution knowledge visible so that s/he might be clearer about the foundations for future problem solving in her/his own life,
- establishing details about what personal resources and knowledges persons relied upon in making the solutions work for them, and
- making these discoveries and knowledges available to others who might be experiencing similar plights.

- *When reviewing your problem-solving capabilities, which of these do you think you could depend on most in the future? Would it be helpful to keep your knowledge of these capabilities alive and well? How could this be done?*
- *Understanding the steps that you took in solving this problem is half of the story. If we could work out how you made this approach work for you, we would understand the other half. What personal and relationship qualities were essential in achieving what you have achieved?*
- *Just imagine that I was meeting with a person who/family that was experiencing a problem like you used to have. From what you know, what advice do you think I could give that person/family?*
- *Let's suppose that someone found out that you were a veteran of this sort of problem and that you had freed your life from it. If they were to consult you, how would you help them?*
- *Most of what therapists know that is useful they learn from working with persons who seek their help. Would you be prepared to support my efforts to preserve knowledges about solving problems so that these might be available to others in the future?*

Unique Account Questions

Unique account questions encourage persons to:
- develop an account of the nature of their solution knowledges - their hard-won know-how, and
- plot the steps that they took in the development of their problem-solving knowledges, as they unfolded through time.

The articulation and naming of these knowledges contributes to their survival and accessibility, and the experience of the unfolding of preferred developments in one's life, through history, appears vital to a positive sense of future.

- *All right, you have given me a summary of what you did. However, this is quite general, and I would be interested in some of the specifics. Would you be prepared to give me a step-by-step description of how you arrived at this?*
- *So what led up to this breakthrough? Tell me about your preparation for this. What advice were you giving to yourself? What did you witness yourself doing that might have been the first step? Did anyone else notice this and, if so, what part did they play?*
- *I now have a reasonable idea of what you did that worked for you. I doubt that this just came out of the blue. What foundation is this approach based upon, and how did you develop it?*
- *What could you tell me about your history that would help me understand the development of your problem-solving abilities?*
- *What would I have witnessed in your life, at an earlier time, that would have enabled me to conclude that you would break free of the problem at this point?*[4]

Unique Redescription Questions

These questions encourage persons to reflect upon the alternative knowledges of self, others, and of relationships that were resurrected and/or generated in the therapy. Attention is directed to the conclusions reached, and realizations had, about the capabilities and competencies of persons and relationships, and about how these capabilities and competencies are reflected in the solution know-how that was employed for dealing with the problem.

As much as possible, these questions historicize these alternative knowledges.
- *As you review the meetings that we have had together, what occurs to you as important realizations about who you are as people, and about the qualities in your relationships?*
- *Over the time that we have been meeting, what have you become clearer about in terms of who you are as a person and about your preferred way of relating to others? What do you now know about what kind of a life suits your sort of person and what doesn't?*
- *Let's consider the steps that you took to achieve this breakthrough. What personal and relationship qualities do you think you were relying on to see this through? Which personal and relationship qualities were most supportive of these steps?*
- *What do these achievements reflect about your lives and relationships that is important for you to know?*
- *What would you conclude about a person who achieved what you have achieved in challenging the problems' influence in your lives?*
- *Having witnessed yourselves take this action, what conclusions have you been able to reach about yourselves and your relationships - conclusions that were not available to you before? What do you now know about yourselves as people that you would not have known otherwise?*
- *Who, from all of those people who have known your past, would have been most likely to have reached similar conclusions about you? What might they have observed about you as a younger person that could have led them to these conclusions?*
- *What do these achievements reflect about the sort of person you are that is important for you to know? Are you the first person to know this about yourself, or have others known this about you in the past? If others have known this, what told them?*

Unique Possibility Questions

These questions encourage persons to speculate about the various options and the possibilities that might accompany a knowledgeable life. This brings forth a discussion of new destinations and futures, and of the specific steps that might be taken to realize these. In general, the questions are future-oriented, with "future-oriented backward-looking" questions strongly featured.[5]

Future-oriented backward-looking questions are those that request persons to imagine themselves arriving at some valued destination in life, and then to look back to the present to determine which of those steps they are taking are most relevant or important to achieving that destination, and to determine what subsequent steps were most helpful in achieving that end.

- *Knowing what you now know about yourself and your preferred way of living, how will this knowledge affect your next step? When you witness yourself taking this step, how do you expect that to influence how you feel? And how do you think this will further influence your view of yourself as a person?*
- *Would you mind if we speculate about what sort of new possibilities accompany these new realizations?*
- *I am becoming aware of a history that is different, in some respects, from the one that you previously had - or at least the one that you thought you had. Would you mind if I ask some questions about the sort of future that it might be bringing with it? How might this new future be different from the future of the other past?*
- *I would like you to imagine that you are now further up the road of life, at some valued destination, and looking back to the present. With the benefit of hindsight, what stands out as the most significant steps that you are taking at the moment, and where did those steps lead to next?*
- *From that vantage point in your future, what new directions were made possible by what you have recently discovered about yourself? How did these realizations and conclusions make it possible for you to intervene in your future, and in what way?*

Circulation Questions

These questions assist persons in the identification and recruitment of appropriate audiences to the performance of solution knowledges, and the alternative knowledges of lives and of relationships. Such audiences play a very significant part in the authentication of the preferred claims that accompany these knowledges.

At this time, the extent to which persons are prepared to make their knowledges accessible to others, who might be experiencing similar

problems, can be ascertained, and the conditions under which this material could be made available to these persons can be determined.
- *Now that you have reached this point in life, who else should know about it? What difference do you think it would make to their attitude towards you if they had this news? What would be the best way of introducing them to this news?*
- *Do you think it would be helpful to catch others up on these developments? If so, how could you engage their interest? What would be most important for them to know?*
- *Since it is important to put others in the know, what might give people a reasonable familiarity with the new realizations and conclusions that you have recently arrived at?*
- *I guess there are a number of people who have an outdated view of who you are as a person. What ideas do you have for updating these views? What would be most newsworthy?*
- *Would it be helpful to go along with others in the illusion that everything is just the same in your life? If not, how could you arrange for others to join you in celebrating your achievement?*
- *If other persons seek therapy for the same reasons that you did, can I share with them any of the important discoveries that you have made? If so, to what extent can I do this, and under what circumstances?*

OWNERSHIP AND USAGE OF DOCUMENTS

We acknowledge that therapeutic productions are co-created, but consider the persons who seek therapy to be the senior partners in the ownership of this property. Thus, such persons have power of veto in relation to the use of any documents (including videotape) produced by their consultancy.

Persons are informed that these documents, which we refer to as archives, are considered to be on loan to the therapist for specific purposes and for specific periods of time, and that this loan can be retracted at any time. Despite this, many persons wish to deed these archives to the therapist to use at his/her discretion.

The therapist may suggest that persons consult the knowledges expressed in their own documents at certain points in time, or request that these documents be made available, with discretion, to others who are experiencing problems or for teaching purposes, with an undertaking that the responses of others will be recorded and made available.

The recording of the responses of participants in teaching contexts, with the explicit goal of providing feedback to those persons whose documents are being presented, encourages these participants to more fully appreciate and respect the nature of their privileged position. This is a position in which participants are privy to the lives and relationships of those persons who have been willing to contribute to the development of "therapeutic knowledge". This recording of responses engages participants more fully in an understanding of the experiences of persons, and mitigates against those responses that are the outcome of a position of detachment that is so easily arrived at by participants in teaching contexts.

Persons are invariably enthusiastic about receiving feedback from others in relation to their therapeutic productions. At times this feedback provokes ongoing and productive correspondences between these persons and workshop participants when these participants have appended an address to their comments.

CONCLUSION

In this paper we have described a process that we would refer to as an "archaeology of therapy". In this process, the knowledges that have been resurrected and/or generated in the context of therapy, and the history of, or conditions that made the production of these knowledges possible, become known. Persons become knowledge-makers, and knowledge-makers become knowledgeable. Both their knowledge-making capabilities and their knowledgeableness are authenticated.

This encourages persons to deploy their knowledges more knowingly, increases their own authority in matters of their concern, and decreases their dependency on expert knowledges. We believe that such knowledges can be more viable, enduring, and efficient than the imported expert knowledges which are often disabling and, in many circumstances, introducing of a stupifying patienthood.

NOTES

1. In challenging this privileging of the therapeutic micro-world we are not proposing that all aspects of therapy be undertaken in some public domain. We believe that persons should have access to a private place in which they can feel safe and secure, and have their desire for confidentiality honoured. However, we consider it inappropriate to place this world above all other worlds, and we believe that all knowledges that arise in therapy that are preferred knowledges for persons should have space made available for the circulation of the same. We prefer to construe the concluding stages of therapy as being about new beginnings.

2. Turner and Hepworth distinguish between two major classes of ritual: those that include persons in social groups, and those that exclude persons from them.

3. In the translation of van Gennep's text, we prefer the term "reincorporation" over the term "reaggregation".

4. These can also be constructed as experience of experience questions (White 1988b). For example, "What would ... (an historically significant person) have noticed that would have told them that you would have been able to achieve this at this point in time?" Daphne Hewson (1990) proposes very similar questions from a cognitive social psychology orientation.

5. Other therapists, including those of varying perspectives, have also concluded that questions of this type are particularly helpful. For example, Daphne Hewson (1990) reaches this conclusion from a cognitive social psychology orientation.

REFERENCES

Douglas, M. 1982:
   In The Active Voice. London; Routledge, Kegan & Paul.
Epston, D. 1985:
   An Interview with David Epston. **Family Therapy Association of South Australia Newsletter**, pp.11-14. (Reprinted in Epston, D. 1989: **Collected Papers**. Adelaide; Dulwich Centre Publications.)
Epston, D. 1987:
   A Reflexion. **Dulwich Centre Newsletter**, Summer, pp.16-17. (Reprinted in Epston, D. 1989: **Collected Papers**. Adelaide; Dulwich Centre Publications.)
Epston, D. & White, M. 1989:
   Literate Means to Therapeutic Ends. Adelaide; Dulwich Centre Publications. (Republished in 1990 by W.W.Norton & Co. under the title **Narrative Means to Therapeutic Ends**.)
Foucault, M. 1973:
   The Birth of the Clinic: An archaeology of medical perception. London; Tavistock.

Geertz, C. 1976:
　From the natives' point of view: On the nature of anthropological understanding. In Basso, K. & Selby, H. (Eds.): **Meaning in Anthropology**. Albuquerque; University of New Mexico Press.

Harre, R. 1983:
　Personal Being: A theory for Individual psychology. Oxford; Blackwell.

Hewson, D. 1991:
　From laboratory to therapy room: Prediction questions for reconstructing the 'new-old' story. **Dulwich Centre Newsletter**, No.3, pp.5-12.

Kobak, R. & Waters, D. 1984:
　Family therapy as a rite of passage: The play's the thing. **Family Process**, 23(1).

Mauss, M. 1954:
　The Gift: Forms and function in archaic societies. London; Cohen & West.

Turner, B. & Hepworth, M. 1982:
　Confession: Studies in deviance in religion. London; Routledge, Kegan & Paul.

Turner, V. 1967:
　The Forest of Symbols: Aspects of Ndembu ritual. Ithaca, NY; Cornell University Press.

Turner, V. 1986:
　Dewey, Dilthey, and drama. In Turner, V. & Bruner, E. (Eds.): **The Anthropology of Experience**. Chicago; University of Illinois Press.

van Gennep, A. 1960:
　The Rite of Passage. Chicago; Chicago University Press.

White, M. 1986:
　Awards and their contribution to change. **Dulwich Centre Newsletter**, May.

White, M. 1988a:
　The process of questioning: A therapy of literary merit. **Dulwich Centre Newsletter**, Winter, pp.8-14. (Reprinted in White, M. 1989: **Selected Papers**. Adelaide; Dulwich Centre Publications.)

White, M. 1988b:
　Saying hullo again: The reincorporation of the lost relationship in the resolution of grief. **Dulwich Centre Newsletter**, Spring, pp.7-11. (Reprinted in White, M. 1989: **Selected Papers**. Adelaide; Dulwich Centre Publications.)

White, M. 1988/89:
　The externalizing of the problem and the re-authoring of lives and relationships. **Dulwich Centre Newsletter**, Summer, pp.3-21. (Reprinted in White, M. 1989: **Selected Papers**. Adelaide; Dulwich Centre Publications.)

White, M. & Epston, D. 1985:
　Consulting your consultant's consultants. In Chable et al. (Eds.): **The Proceedings of the Sixth Australian Family Therapy Conference**. Melbourne; Victorian Association of Family Therapy.

White, M. & Epston, D. 1989:
　Literate Means to Therapeutic Ends. Adelaide; Dulwich Centre Publications. (Republished as **Narrative Means to Therapeutic Ends**. New York; W.W.Norton.)

CHAPTER II

a conversation about
AIDS AND DYING

with

Michael White & David Epston

*Previously published in
Dulwich Centre Newsletter
1991, No.2.*

About two years ago, while sitting in a garden on a fine day in spring, Cheryl White interviewed David Epston and me about our ideas in relation to working with persons who were dying. She requested that we focus particularly on gay persons who had contracted HIV, and who had developed AIDS. Cheryl asked that we endeavour to reproduce this discussion for this issue of the Newsletter. Rather than interview us again, it was her preference that David and I engage each other in a discussion of the ideas that we exchanged in that earlier interview. What follows is a transcript of that more recent discussion. We would like to thank Cheryl for encouraging us to do this. If it had not been for her searching questions, in the first place, around what we believed were heartening ways of working with persons who are dying, we would not have thought through the practices discussed here at all well, and certainly would not have articulated them in this way.

Michael White

Michael: *David, in response to the questions that Cheryl originally posed for us, I recall that you talked about some of the work that you had been doing around talking with people about how they would like to live on in the memories of their relatives, friends and acquaintances. Obviously you have found this notion of the continuity of one's life to be a fairly significant issue for persons who are dying.*

David: *Yes, I have.*

Michael: *Could you talk some about that?*

David: *The importance of this idea came to me partly through my experience of working with persons who were dying, and partly through my reading about mortuary rituals - in fact cross-cultural studies of mortuary rituals. I was doing this reading in response to your work on the "saying hullo" metaphor and the "reincorporation of the lost relationship" (White 1988). One feature of these mortuary rituals that is very apparent is the distinction drawn around the death of the body and the survival of the personhood of the deceased.*

Experience, Contradiction, Narrative & Imagination

Michael: *This is a very interesting distinction, perhaps one that suggests considerable awareness of the extent to which a person's "self" is social, of the extent to which one's sense of personhood is negotiated and distributed within a community of persons. Would you give me an example of the actual practices associated with this distinction?*

David: *Well, the distinction is usually drawn across time. At a particular point in time after the ritualized goodbye to the dead body, the relatives of the bereaved assemble again, this time to take on the virtues of the deceased, or, if you like, the spirit of the deceased. Perhaps we could say that, at this time, the spirit of the deceased is regained.*

Michael: *Would you give me an account of one of these rituals?*

David: *Right. Let's take voodoo. From this reading I became aware of the extent to which certain forms of voodoo have been misrepresented in popular culture. For example, one practice of voodoo is for the family and friends of the deceased to gather and to conceive of themselves in the image of the horse, and to imagine themselves to be mounted by the virtues of the deceased. Thus, from there on, to an extent at least, these relatives and friends experience their lives to be ridden by these virtues. This really reinforced my interest in rethinking the "therapy" of those who are dying.*

Michael: *Okay, let's talk about some of the actual practices of therapy that would interact with these ideas.*

David: *Let me begin by talking about working with the bereaved. I started asking bereaved persons questions like: "Of all the virtues of your dead sister Rosemary, which of these would you like to carry forward in your own life?", and "Do you think, by doing this, that you will be able to keep her memory alive?" So, I was thinking about how therapy might contribute to keeping memories alive. And from there I went on to the idea of asking the dying person about how they would like their "legacy" to live on.*

Michael: *This really fits with my experience of meeting with dying persons. I often find that persons have been reflecting, in one way or another, on what piece, if any, of their life will survive physical death. And so often this* question is posed in terms of "contribution". For example: "Did I make any enduring contribution?"; "What did my life amount to?"; "What has been my significance to the lives of other persons?"

David: *It is not a question that is very often taken up by others or addressed all that well.*

Michael: *No, it isn't. And perhaps this relates to our culture's emphasis on material existence.*

David: *I think the word "legacy" is a good word for us to think more about. In fact this word was offered by Cheryl during our previous discussion of this issue. I like to think that the person's personhood is the legacy of the person.*

Michael: *And we know that this personhood is a deeply significant legacy to those who have experienced loss, deeply significant to their sense of well-being.*

David: *Yes. I recall being consulted by a woman whose best friend had died. This woman was feeling very confused and was clearly aggrieved - and had been so for quite some time. On remembering her friend, she said that she felt she "had lost her right hand". I asked her some of the "saying hullo" questions, and later, when she returned, she described her friend as "my right arm". In a manner of speaking, she redescribed her friend as embodied in her. She had taken the personhood of this friend into her body, and was no longer experiencing the confusion and the grief.*

Michael: *I would refer to this as a reincorporation, because I suspect that the woman's experience of her friend's experience was a vital part of the woman's life when her friend was alive.*

David: *Yes, it is through these questions that the lost other is re-internalized.*

Michael: *So, we know that a person's personhood is not extinguished by physical death. We know that this personhood can and does live on in the lives of those who were significant to them - lives on as it always did in the same community of persons in which it was negotiated in the first place. And* we know that this personhood can be very enriching of the lives of others in that community. How could this understanding influence the work done with persons who are dying?

David: *Your question leads me to a consideration of testamentary practices - for example those that relate to the writing of a will. A will usually has to do with the dispersal of property. Now, on drawing a distinction around material property and personal virtues, or, as some might prefer, spiritual property, the will becomes a cultural prototype for the dispersal of personhood. What do you think of that?*

Michael: *Great! This other will would authorize the existence of personhood beyond physical existence.*

David: *Some of my reading suggests this could be particularly relevant, because many AIDS sufferers are dying "too young". And there isn't a precedent for this in modern western culture. I think that the idea of the dying person as a benefactor and of inviting certain persons to be the beneficiaries goes some way towards addressing this issue.*

Michael: *I believe that once persons have been assisted to identify their contribution to other people's lives, the formalization of this in the way of a will, as you suggest, would be a very significant ritual.*

David: *I was working with a woman who was terminally ill. Shortly before her death she made me the agent of her will and testament. As part of my duties as agent, it was my responsibility to distribute, to appropriate persons, copies of a very important document. This document included a testimony to the sexual abuse that she had experienced as a young person, some thoughts about how others might free themselves from the long term effects of such abuse, and a message of hope.*

Michael: *Now you are talking about the person's contribution to the lives of others in another way. You are talking about how persons might be engaged in passing on their special knowledges to others, or, if you like, some of their accumulated wisdom. So that these special knowledges might be circulated. These special knowledges could include alternative knowledges about ways of* being in certain communities, like in the gay community - alternative knowledges about life and about relationships, about solving problems, about the resolution of certain dilemmas, and so on.

David: *And about courage and about dying.*

Michael: *And about alternative knowledges of self.*

David: *In what sense do you mean "alternative knowledges of self"?*

Michael: *When Cheryl interviewed us, she asked what we thought were special issues for dying persons who had been marginalized. This had me thinking about some of the dying persons who had consulted me. Those of this group who had experienced marginalization in their families, social groups, places of work or culture, had responded very positively to questions that invited them to review and/or revision the meaning of their lives. And even many of those who had not been so marginalized have been interested in reviewing the meaning of their lives at this time.*

David: *When you refer to meaning, do you mean purpose?*

Michael: *Yes, purpose. But not "purpose" in a philosophical sense like "what was it all for?". I am talking more about the purposes or intentions or motives that persons ascribe to their actions in the course of their own lives, and I am talking about the review or revision of these historical meanings.*

David: *Go ahead ...*

Michael: *Well, let's take persons who have been marginalized. It is not at all unusual for such persons to have a private story about being unworthy, about failing to measure-up in some way or another. Although at times these private stories are masked by bravado, they are often experienced as total. However, despite this, the very marginalized position of such persons is a fact that can provide a gateway to an alternative story of who they might be. For example, gay persons can be encouraged to give an account of the turning points in their lives - turning points at which they made decisions that they knew they would be derided for, or for which they would be discriminated*

Experience, Contradiction, Narrative & Imagination

against. Such decisions include those that relate to the nature of their sexual desire and, more generally, to their sexual identity and preferred lifestyle. These decisions inevitably constitute a protest, a point of resistance to accepted ways of being in this world, and mark the entry into relatively uncharted territories.

David: *Okay, I'm clear about how the development of such an account serves the purpose of challenging these highly negative and totalizing stories. Would you care to say a little more about how this relates to the revision of meaning?*

Michael: *Sure. Once these alternative accounts have been sufficiently articulated, it becomes possible to pose questions that invite a review or a revision of purpose. This is a review, in the light of the alternative account, of what the person was trying for in his or her life. To respond to these questions is to think about life as a project or a commitment, one shaped by certain desires and beliefs - by desires and beliefs of a nature that suffering could not overwhelm. By the way, this revision of purpose is not to be mistaken for a palliative. It is not based on a specious account of the person's history. As I have stated, it is based on an alternative account, and an alternative account is just that - an alternative account.*

David: *So what questions would you be asking?*

Michael: *For example I might ask the person to reflect on the alternative account by asking questions like: "What do you think this says about what you were trying to do with your life?"; or "What does this reflect about what you intended for your life?"; or "What does this suggest about what you believed your life should be?"; and so on.*

David: *I can see how responding to such questions could be a powerful and refreshing experience for persons with what our culture constructs as "spoiled identities".*

Michael: *Yes, like gay persons with AIDS. There has been so much moralizing around the issue of AIDS. For example, those victims who are not gay or intravenous drug users are commonly referred to as the "innocent" victims.*

Aids & Dying

David: *The history of the discovery of AIDS supports what you are saying about this moralizing. It was considered to be a gay issue, and for a considerable time more money was poured into the research on Legionnaires Disease when there had been something like 129 victims.*

Michael: *Let's get back to our discussion of some of the practices that relate to the revision of meaning.*

David: *Okay.*

Michael: *A community of persons can be invited to join in this activity. For example, any sympathetic relatives, friends and acquaintances can be encouraged to contribute to the alternative account, and to reflect on what this says about the plans that the dying persons had for their life - about what they desired for their lives, about what they were committed to, or, perhaps, what it says about their life as a "work". And the experience of others who cannot be physically present, but who might be considered significant, can be evoked as well. Here the "saying hullo" questions are very helpful.*

David: *Do you mean in terms of engaging the "personhood" of others now deceased - of others who may have been significant to the dying person, or who, on reflection, might be historically significant to the dying person?*

Michael: *Exactly. I was thinking of the extent to which those dying persons who are interested in the review and/or revision of meaning in their lives can be encouraged to identify certain historical figures who might be significant to them - significant to them because they also challenged accepted ways of being in life, and also entered some uncharted territory. Maybe a figure who took risks to make a life of their own with little if any support, and who was prepared to pay the price for this, in terms of suffering and so on. Or maybe a figure who did something entirely different.*

David: *Give me an example.*

Michael: *I know a gay person with AIDS whose parents migrated from Europe at enormous risk and who, with little, if any, support, endured great hardship in their project of re-establishing their lives.*

David: *Are you thinking only of relatives or forebears?*

Michael: *No. It may be a figure that the person has some historical association with, or a figure with whom the person experiences a particular affinity. Once identified, the "personhood" of these figures can be evoked through "saying hullo" questions or "experience of experience questions", and this can play a significant part in revisions of meaning, or purpose. The dying person can be invited to enter an experience of the historical figure's experience of them, through remembering, imagining and speculation. An example of the sort of question that would encourage this is: "Tell me, if you were reviewing this account of your life through this person's eyes right now, what conclusions would you come to about your intentions for your life, intentions that this person could have appreciated?"*

David: *As you have been talking, I've been thinking of the sort of questions that could be asked that might assist in the identification of such figures. I came up with: "If you looked back over the history of your life, who else did you know who may have pioneered a geographical, intellectual, emotional or social territory?" This figure would not necessarily have to be one who would exactly agree with the decisions that the dying person had made about their life, but someone who might appreciate the spirit of these decisions.*

Michael: *Yes. This discussion takes us back to the subject of the legacy. Perhaps these practices that relate to the revision of purpose lend some clarity to the nature of the legacy itself. Perhaps it is time to wrap up this discussion with some final comments, and then get back to Cheryl to ask her whether she thinks we have captured the essence of the earlier interview.*

David: *Okay. A last comment. I think we could all go a lot further in terms of exploring the distinctions that have been drawn in mortuary rituals, and to encourage persons to think about personhood as a legacy. If what we are defining as personhood lives on in the lives of others as we know it does, then we could be a lot more interested in establishing the sort of conditions around the dying person that would enable them to have a lot more to say about how this legacy will be distributed or dispersed. I am sure that all of those who decided to participate in establishing such conditions would find it "enlivening".*

Michael: *And I would just like to say that for many persons who are dying, and particularly for those who have been marginalized by our culture through the ascription of "spoiled identities", that this time can provide them with an opportunity to become more active in, or to have a more major say in, the authorship of their own lives - perhaps to take over the authorship of their own lives - and to discover, in the process, that they are persons to be treasured. This time also can provide an opportunity for these persons to have the experience of a particular sense of presence in a community of persons, and perhaps even a community of "spirits" - of a unique sense of place in the world and of a unique sense of connectedness.*

REFERENCE

White, M. 1988:
Saying hullo again: The reincorporation of the lost relationship in the resolution of grief. **Dulwich Centre Newsletter**, Spring, pp.7-11. (Reprinted in White, M. 1989, **Selected Papers**. Adelaide; Dulwich Centre Publications.)

CHAPTER III

TEMPER TANTRUM PARTIES:
Saving face, losing face, or going off your face![1]

David Epston

Previously published in
Dulwich Centre Newsletter
Autumn 1989.

Temper Tantrum Parties is an original method of therapeutic intervention for 'out of control' behaviours involving uncontrolled anger. This approach can be utilized with children from the age of eight or nine, adolescents, and adults, and has been extensively applied to presentations of 'out of control' behaviours in children and adolescents. Hitherto, many of these young people were either institutionalized or placed in residential care where such behaviours were contained and controlled by others. Thus, control-by-others had often been substituted for self-control in the lives of these children and adolescents. The approach is simple, economical, and frequently very amusing for all concerned, and I do not believe that it is, in any way, coercive or degrading.

MAKING THE DISCOVERY[2]

The supervisor of another agency had called me several times to detail the urgency of the Moore family's crisis.[3] Mr Brown had abandoned the family when his de-facto wife of three years was in the advanced stages of an unplanned pregnancy, one that he had insisted go to term. Mrs Moore had then given birth and, after much agonizing about adoption, had decided to keep the baby. In addition, her 15 year old daughter, Noelene, had recently had an abortion and Mrs Moore took the blame for "setting a bad example". Mrs Moore was currently under tremendous pressure, holding down a full-time job, caring for a colicky, night-waking infant up to 8 times per night, and coping with Noelene's rebelliousness.

Mrs Moore complained that she could not get any co-operation from Noelene and her son, Wayne, aged 13 years. Typically she would make a request of her children; this would be rejected and then she would attempt to punish them for not complying with the request by resentfully doing the task herself. It infuriated her but this went unnoticed by both Noelene and Wayne. Also, Mrs Moore explicitly expected Noelene to provide her with friendship and company; but Noelene preferred her boyfriend.

We worked together in the first session to reorganize some of the household tasks. Noelene was absent for the second session. Mrs Moore reported that family matters had improved markedly although relations between herself and Noelene had remained strained. By my calculations, Mrs Moore was working between 16-20 hours per day in her salaried job, in the provision of child care, in domestic work, and in the servicing of Noelene's demands. In addition, to make ends meet, she was now considering a part-time cleaning job. Mrs Moore believed that this additional employment had become necessary because Noelene refused to take into account the family's financial straits. Earlier on the day of our second meeting, Mrs Moore had failed to fit her house key into the lock on the first try and fell to the ground crying. There she had remained for some time until discovered by Wayne.

I warned against the idea of additional work as I regarded her to be on the verge of physical collapse. Mrs Moore then told me that she could no longer face Noelene's tantrumming. Apparently, Noelene would tantrum if Mrs Moore did not immediately satisfy her demands to clean, wash, and iron for her. In addition, Mrs Moore was required to prepare meals for Noelene's boyfriend and his friends almost every night, and to wash up after them.

I immediately arranged another meeting and requested that Noelene attend. I had no clear idea of what I might do, but I knew that it was urgent that something be done to relieve Mrs Moore of this pressure. Noelene prepared herself for the interview by having her boyfriend, Peter, join us. I welcomed him, and some time later asked if he had ever seen Noelene's tantrums. He laughed, saying that it was inconceivable that she would do that in his presence. I suspect that Noelene was very embarrassed by the discussion as I found it impossible to engage her. I purposefully misheard the few responses that she gave to my questions. I often do this with mumbling, shy, or unwilling adolescents:

Noelene: (Mumbling inaudibly in response to DE's question.)
DE: (Incredulously) *You want to buy a pumpkin?*
Noelene: (Looking at me in amazement.) *What do you mean pumpkin?*
DE: *I thought you said you wanted to buy a pumpkin.*
Noelene: (Laughing, but now perfectly audible and responsive.) *No ... what I said was ...*

Throughout the interview I persistently regained her attention to further references to pumpkins or by queries about pumpkin pies. The following account of our discussion illustrates this technique:
"Have you ever tried pumpkin pie? You know, I was born in Canada and pumpkin pies are more or less the national dish. They are very delicious!"
Noelene informed me that she had never eaten pumpkin pie and had only

eaten it as a boiled or roasted vegetable. I commiserated with her: *"That's too bad. You ought to try pumpkin pie some time. It's the Canadian national dish."* Further non-sequiturs were around variations on pumpkin pies: *"Have you ever tried pumpkin pie with whipped cream on it? It's even better than just pumpkin pie on its own."* Bemused, Noelene would reply: *"Well, no, how could I? I've only ever eaten pumpkin as a vegie."* My response was: *"This is very sad, Noelene. You're really missing out on something."* Some time later, I enquired: *"Have you ever had pumpkin pie with whipped cream on it and rum in it?"* Again, her attention was rivetted, and she became very involved with our discussion, as did Peter.

I finally connected pumpkin pie eating and the variable geography of her tantrumming into an intervention which Noelene agreed to. This intervention made it possible for the problem-free context (her social space shared with Peter and other age-mates) to intrude upon the problem-context (her social space shared with her mother and sibling). The following is my written summary of this intervention.

Dear Friends,

I know that temper tantrums can be embarrassing for all concerned. For this reason I agreed to draw up a temper trantrum programme that will help matters. In return, Noelene, you agreed to make a tape with me and your family, if you go a month without a tantrum.

1. *It is a good thing for mothers and daughters to have a good argument every so often. How else can you sort things out?*
2. *Temper tantrums are juvenile. A temper tantrum equals 'if you don't let me do what I want' or 'if you don't do what I want, I'll have a temper tantrum'.*
3. *Both Noelene and her mother assured me that you would prefer arguments to temper tantrums.*
4. *Here's how you do it:*

TEMPER TANTRUM CONTROL PROGRAMME

A. *Mother is to make large cards with:*
   1. *I think you've got a temper tantrum coming on.*
   2. *Pre-recording Warning No.1*
   3. *Pre-recording Warning No.2*
   4. *Final Pre-recording Warning*

Have them ready at all times.

B. *As soon as a good argument degenerates, hold up Card No.1. If Noelene exercises self-control, thank her. Then have time out (say ten minutes) before you resume the argument or leave it if feelings are running too high. If she continues, hold up warnings at one minute intervals. This means that she will have three minutes to tantrum. After Final Pre-recording Warning, start recording her temper tantrum on a cassette recorder. Saying nothing; just keep out of the way and record.*

C. *Have Noelene sign, in advance, copies of this sample letter:*
Dear Lewis/Carl/David,

I would like to invite you and Peter to my house on ... (include time and date), to have a piece of pumpkin pie and whipped cream and listen to a recording. I will be disappointed if you can't come.
Love, Noelene.

D. *Ask Peter to deliver these letters if necessary and to make the arrangements.*

E. *Noelene, if there is a dispute in which you and your mother cannot negotiate a compromise and you think a referee would help, ring me.*

Good luck for a temper-tantrum-free month! Please ring me and let me know the result.
Yours sincerely, DE.

One month later Noelene informed me that she could now make her temper-tantrum-free tape. The following excerpts are from the transcript of the audio-tape.

DE: *Well, we met a month ago and Noelene, you and I made a deal that if you had a temper-tantrum-free month you and I and your family would make a tape. I'd like to know about your temper tantrums because you told me you had a pretty serious sort of problem. You described your problem as out of your control.*

Noelene: *I can control it now. I don't get so mad. I don't shout any more or scream at Mum.*

DE: *Do you miss her screaming?*

Mrs.M: *It's lovely and peaceful.*

Wayne: *She's still got a loud voice though.*

Mrs.M: *But who hasn't? Everyone has at certain times.* (To DE) *It's much better.*

DE: *How much difference has it made to you as a family?*

Mrs.M: *We're all getting on better. We're not living in fear that if we say*

anything wrong she will flare up and slam the doors and scream and shout.
DE: *Were you afraid of her before?*
Mrs.M: *Not afraid; it upset me. I don't know ... just the thought there could be a ...*
DE: *Tantrum?*
Mrs.M: *So I would just be more careful what I said.*
DE: *Then you're watching what you're saying, so there's tension all the time?*
Wayne: *She hasn't had a tempter tantrum in ages.*
DE: *Are you a bit sad about that? Are you missing them? You know - some people like them.*
Wayne: *No!*
DE: *Okay, how did you do it? How did you come to control them? Of all the things in the Temper Tantrum Control Programme, what do you think were the things that helped you control them?*
Wayne: *I know what: I know what it was. Me and Peter stirred her up about it. We said that you'll have to have your friends around here ...*
Mrs.M: *To listen to that dreadful noise.*
Noelene: (Guffawing)
Wayne: *Whenever we thought she was going to get mad we stirred her up ...*
(general laughter)
Mrs.M: *We'd say 'temper tantrum' and that was enough.*
DE: *Really!*
Noelene: *Yeah!* (followed by general laughter)
DE: *And what would you do then? Instead of having your temper tantrum?*
Noelene: *I'd go off into my bedroom and do something. I'd cool off and come on out.*
DE: *That seems like a pretty reasonable solution. There's nothing wrong with being angry.*
Mrs.M: *Yeah ... It clears the air.*
Noelene: *We get on better ... we discuss things instead of getting into big arguments which cause more trouble.*
DE: *Have you got any advice to give to expressive young women like yourself who have temper tantrum problems? If someone came up to you and said: "I heard through the grapevine that you didn't use to have control over your temper and a month later you did. Would you teach me how to do it?" How would you teach her?*
Noelene: *By getting a tape recording of it and playing it back to their friends.*

Experience, Contradiction, Narrative & Imagination

And then when you feel like getting mad, go for a walk or something and cool off and come back.
DE: *That's a reasonable idea!*
Mrs.M: *If you've got no-one to listen to you, it's not worth having one.*
DE: *Yes. There is a rule of temper tantrums. The rule of temper tantrums is: Temper Tantrums need an audience.*
Mrs.M: *I found once I ignored her ... it helped! She didn't want to carry on. She couldn't be bothered walking after me around the house* (general laughter) ... *"Stay here Mum!" she'd say* ... *"Stay here!" Isn't that right?*
Noelene: *Yeah!* (general laughter)

BACKGROUND

In order to make this approach clinically relevant to practitioners, I will focus on a step-by-step detailed description of both the variable and consistent elements.[4] Although the intervention is discussed in terms of its pragmatics, it is not a 'programme' in the behaviour modification sense of that word. I strive never to allow the common experiences of the tantrummers and their families to obscure the uniqueness of the problem context and the particulars of the experiences of the individuals concerned. The mode of description will be a 'typification' rather than a blanket prescription.

However, some elements of the intervention are, in fact, regularly used, and these will be identified in the text. Although I have set out the steps of the intervention in an orderly fashion, in practice, these steps are not so ordered. They are introduced, re-introduced, and braided together into an assemblage, the purpose of which becomes clear in the later composition of the Letters of Invitation. In judging the suitability of such an approach, it is of vital importance that the therapist scrupulously distinguish families tyrannized by tantrumming from those families in which a young person's outbursts of anger represent a legitimate rebellion against sexual, physical, or emotional abuse. In the second case, to quell such anger would be a gross misapplication of the approach.

Throughout the article, I use the term temper tantrums to describe 'out-of-control' behaviours in general. These behaviours range from 'paddies' to armed assault.[5] I do so for two reasons: firstly as a matter of convenience and, secondly, this relabels the behaviours as age-inappropriate transgressions.[6]

RECONSTRUCTION OF THE PROBLEM

Shared Victimhood

This approach examines the problem in the context of family interaction, and draws a parallel between the temper's tyrannical relationship to the young person **and** the temper's tyrannical relationship to other family members. All are construed as victims of temper with each person suffering in his/her own particular way. Direct or indirect questions[7] are asked about the effect of the temper on them and their relationships. Contrary to what is commonly expected, these questions usually establish that the temper tantrummer is the person who is most victimized, preyed upon, or duped. Other family members come a close second, often living under a reign of terror in homes that have become occupied by the tyranny of temper. All family members, including the temper tantrummer, are joined in an easy and unexpected alliance on the basis of their shared predicament. This alliance rapidly undermines the customary adversarial relationship between the tantrummer and family.

Commonly, parents seek therapy with the hope that it could contribute to their efforts to oppose the young person and his/her tantrumming. Referral often takes place when the 'out-of-control' behaviour is escalated by one perceptible step, such as from tantrumming to violence against property, from violence against property to violence against person(s), or from violence against persons to armed assault. The parents have often reached the conclusion that 'it's either him/her or us' and are considering a solution that requires either the tantrummer's exile from the family or self-exile. More often it is mothers who consider self-exile. These mothers have been so affected by mother-blaming[8] or the tantrummers' 'gas-lighting'[9] that they have come to regard themselves as failures as persons, and some consider suicide or admission into a psychiatric hospital for repair as the only way out. Usually, the tantrummer is convinced that if his/her parents or siblings didn't make any demands, then there would be no trouble.

When a construction of shared victimhood is established, a new 'conversation' is developed, one that is at variance with the habitual conversation through which the tantrummer and his/her family have made sense of their circumstances. The therapist initiates questions that invite family members to participate in this new conversation. The tantrummer frequently defers his/her response to these questions until s/he feels joined by the therapist. Eventually the tantrummer, family, and therapist are arrayed in a conceptual space alongside each other with the temper as their adversary. A preliminary summary at the end of the first or second session might appear something like this:

Jack,

It seems to me that you are being driven into a life of irresponsibility by your temper. It has gotten the better of you and is making you appear silly and immature to others. Tantrumming is to be expected of a much younger person, say aged 3 or 4. I think it is quite unfair and mean that you have become enslaved by your feelings and put under their domination. Would you like to have more influence over yourself and, by doing so, weaken the hold it has had on you for so long now? Do you know that if you strengthen yourself you would weaken your temper by doing so?

Mr & Mrs R,

It saddens me to see such giving people being taken in by tantrumming. Your home has become an occupied zone with all of you living in terror, not knowing what is going to happen next. His temper's tyranny cannot endure for very much longer. Right now, you are very likely plotting its downfall behind closed doors, even though Jack must guess you are talking about him. If you overthrow the temper's tyranny, you will once again be free people and Jack will repossess himself. Do you consider you are entitled to lives free of fear? Do you think Jack deserves to be captured by his feelings?

Externalizing the Problem

The perceived locus of any problem, whether this be situated internally or externally, is culturally arbitrary.[10] For particular problems such loci can vary across cultures and over time within a culture. Recent practices in Western psychologies require a professional to administer treatment to a problem understood to be located within a person. Michael White (1984, 1985, 1986a, 1986b, 1988, 1988/89; Epston & White 1989a, 1989b) has developed a counter-cultural approach which externalizes problems, resulting in a radically different stance by all concerned. The 'sufferer' becomes active in assuming control over his/her problem and its effects on their life and relationships with others (Tomm 1989). An externalized construction of the problem reduces the likelihood of debilitating guilt and self-blame for the 'defect' in the person, and invites agency on the part of the problem-affected person and family.

What is entailed is a rigorous and careful 'conceptual dissection' of the problem, "cutting it away" from the person's sense of self as a person. That is, there is a systematic separation of problematic attributes, ideas, assumptions, beliefs, habits, attitudes, and lifestyles from the patient's dominant identity. (Tomm 1989)

In the case of tantrumming, the problem is conceptually relocated beyond the person. In fact, the temper is radically split away from the self and it is no longer viewed as a constituent part of the person, but an 'occupier', 'possesser', 'capturer', 'invader', etc. And the temper's invasion of the person is considered as unjust and unfair. This motivates the person and family to reclaim themselves from the hold that the problem may have had over them. Such metaphors permit the tantrummer and his/her family to consider that the problem has acted against each and every one of them in ways that they had not previously suspected. A behavioural description or psychological construct - depending on the family's language use - is materialized into an object, thus reifying the problem. A further element of externalizing the problem is that the metaphorical object is personified and provided with the attributes of one or more of the following personae; a ruthless despot, a malicious trickster, a rogue having a joke at the young person's expense, a bully appropriating the young person's dignity for its own selfish ends. Which personae I employ depends very much on the circumstances.

- *Do you think your temper is tricking you or treating you? Do you think you're being treated when it looks like you are being tricked out of your family? Do your parents believe they are treating you into your family while, at the same time, your temper is tricking you out of it?*
- *Why do you think your tantrumming would want you to appear younger than your true age? What advantage would it get over you? Do you think it is right that your temper should steal your maturity behind your back?*
- *How much can you speak your own mind with your tantrumming taking it over and turning you into its lackey? Do you think it's time to win yourself*

back? Who will get the last laugh: you or your tantrumming?

Gradually a contest emerges between the victimized tantrummer and his/her tyrannizing temper. The outcome will be decided in a contest in which the young person either reclaims his/her anger/feelings, or further permits their temper "to have its way with you, keeping in mind what you now know". Other family members are questioned as to their willingness to take their child's side against their common enemy - the tyranny they are all living under. This is what White refers to as ... *pitting the family against the symptom* (1984, pp.153-154), and is unlike the structure of many psychodynamic interventions that pit the child (with the therapist's assistance) against his/her parents, or those behavioural interventions that pit the parents (with the assistance of the therapist) against their child.[11]

In a family with a precocious tantrummer - Keri Moyle, aged 9 years, who was threatening violence - the interviewer[12] only had the opportunity in the first interview to get as far as the introduction of the split between the person and the problem through its externalization. At the second session, two weeks later, Mr and Mrs Moyle reported a dramatic reduction in Keri's tantrumming. They accounted for their success in the following way.

Linden: *It was nice to have the language to use. It's taken the threat away from Keri and put it on her temper. I was getting at the temper and not at my daughter and felt good about it. It was the fact that there was a third entity - the fact that there was something outside of her I could get at. I took control of the temper and not Keri. Before, I saw myself getting at the temper through Keri. Now, Keri was on my side getting rid of the temper. I was able to say to her, 'you or I will take control of it, but our family won't be controlled! As sure as eggs this temper isn't going to be the boss of our family'. She was given the choice of participating or not, but we can now cut her off from it and deal with her temper. The difference was the divorcing of her and her temper.*

Richard: *I think the principle had an appeal for Keri ... she could understand it.*

The Severity of the Problem

The severity of the problem is established by a careful reckoning of its history in the life of the family and its current influence on the

Temper Tantrum Parties

tantrummer's and family members' lives. I acquire rather specific information as to how much time is being taken up by the problem:
How much time do you figure your mother/father/siblings spend(s) a day being afraid of your temper? How much time do you figure s/he is being dominated by his/her temper per day?

The influence of the problem over social relationships can be established by closeness/distance questioning:
As his/her tempers get more violent, do you think his/her mother/father/ siblings are getting closer to him/her or further away? As your tempers get more violent, do you think your mother/etc. is getting more afraid or less fearful of you?

The history of the problem is examined with the purpose of identifying any beliefs that might block the discovery of new solutions. If the tantrumming hasn't been going on for as long as a family can remember, it is useful to enquire as to its commencement and as to the family's understanding of this. Often the tantrumming is accounted for and 'blamed on' an event in the young person's life, e.g. parents' separation, childhood illness, moving school, etc. This may have produced a theory of psychological disability, one that exempts the young person from the expectation of self-control. A careful incident analysis can undermine such ideas. This incident analysis usually identifies the fact that tantrums are sequentially related to the parents' request for co-operation, their denial of a demand made by the young person, or to the parents' desire to state their own opinion:
Are you allergic to the word 'no'? Do you think all your problems would go away if your parents took all the blame for them? ... If your parents retired from acting as your parents? ... If your parents pretended not to be your parents?

Persistently labelling the young person's behaviour as 'temper-tantrum/tantrumming' also ties the behaviours to notions of age-inappropriateness rather than psychological distress or 'frustration'. Even if the problem appeared to start as a fairly obvious situational reaction, I have found it extremely useful to bring the tantrumming under the young person's and family control before discussing these origins at any length. This interrupts the escalating anger-fear cycle, and dramatically initiates a trend towards the perception and construction of a new solution and the repair of relationships. It is also helpful to have family members predict the direction they expect their lives, and that of the young person, to take as or if 's/he comes more under the influence of his/her temper?' If their forecast presumes a growing out of it 'by nature' or that 'it's so bad it can't get any worse', I firmly challenge this on the basis of my experience with the life cycle of tantrumming:

How much do you weigh? Eight stone? He's only having an eight stone tantrum. With practice s/he will increase his/her capacity for it and tolerance to it. This may be just a preview of what's to come. What do you think the main feature will be like?

I also inform myself of the sequence of events surrounding the problem by scrupulously tracking an episode of tantrumming that is fresh in the family's mind. Rather than selecting out extraordinary incidences, I check to see that those related are typical. If this appears to be so contentious that a further imbroglio threatens, then it is unwise to proceed with this discussion.

Simplicity of the Solution

It is then pertinent to draw a dramatic distinction between the problem and its severity on the one hand, and the solution in its simplicity on the other. The solution is imputed to be simple, in fact, surprisingly so:
Look, I've met 36 temper tantrummers before today, and you know, everyone of them, except two, turned their back on a temper tantrumming lifestyle.

I might describe what happened with these two exceptions and propose that the successful solution on these occasions was undone by some restraint. This I would do if I had a hunch that a similar restraint was operating in the family I was currently interviewing:
It worked for five months with one young person but then she decided to ring up her father every time she didn't get her own way. Her parents had been separated for some time but her mother mistakenly believed that the separation was her fault even though he ran off with another woman. How crazy can you get? Guilt once again overtook the mother and the temper took over her daughter.
I then ask: *Do you believe me?*

Following this, I invite family members into a discussion about how those families that were successful achieved what they did. Following this, I ask: *How long do you think it took them?*

Temper Tantrum Parties

Such a question evolves a temporal context for the events to come, and lends a different complexion to considerations about the properties of persons and the explanations for temper tantrumming. Family members usually respond by guessing anywhere between two months and one year, or with the more indefinite 'ages'. In the face of these predictions, family members usually find my response quite startling:

One session - matter of fact, they walked out the door there (pointing) and their temper never got the better of them again. They tell me something happened just about the second step down on their way out. A number have marked the spot with an x. Would you be interested in seeing their marks? I can't make any sense of it - they say something about feeling vibrations.

After the interview, on the way out, I often take young tantrummers (aged 8-12 years) aside and show them the marks and ask them to stand on the most recent one. Many of them report that they can feel something, and I then endeavour to get precise details:

Did the vibrations stop at your ankle or go right up to your knee? Were they ticklish? Do you feel stronger or weaker now?

For young people, this offers a magical explanation and empowerment for the contest ahead. It also locates a solution in some action taken by the young person.

For adolescents and their parents, I provide all concerned with the opportunity for either (1) having post-treatment letters from parents or ex-temper tantrummers read aloud to them, or (2) calling up veterans against temper tantrumming who have willingly agreed to remain on phone duty to offer support and reassurances about the simplicity of the solution, or (3) listening to or watching audio or audio-video tapes of ex-temper tantrummers and their families telling of their victories over the influence of tantrums in their lives. The following is an example of a post-treatment letter from parents to other parents. I also have a collection from ex-tantrummers themselves and can usually find an age-appropriate one for all new referrals.

CASE VIGNETTE

Chloe (aged 13 years) was extremely advanced for her age. She had been tantrumming for the past four years and this was on the increase. Her parents had become quite frightened by the lengths to which she would go in these tantrums.

The family was sent a reasonable facsimile of the letter referred to when discussing the Moore family. Chloe's letter read:
I would like to invite you to my house on .... (time and date) for a Temper Tantrum and Pumpkin Pie Party. Pumpkin pie and whipped cream will be provided by my friend, David. He has agreed to do this because he has failed to help me. I will play you a recording of my tantrumming so you can help me change. I will be deeply hurt if you don't come to my party.

If necessary, this letter was to be delivered by her younger brother to her three best friends. In addition, I included a confidential letter to Chloe:
Dear Chloe,

I may be wrong in expecting you to grow up before your time. After all, you are between being a young girl and a young woman. If you decide to grow up I want to warn you that you will have to leave the fun and games of childhood behind - Enid Blyton books, hopscotch, building sand castles, and so many other things kids like to do. It's a big decision. If you decide not to grow up I will still respect you and find another way to help. DE

The following was also appended to the 'temper tantrum control programme' letter:
It struck all of us that Chloe has a lot of concerns for a girl her age. For some reason or other, she has been under the impression that her worries will overwhelm her parents. It was agreed that her father would provide her with a daily scheduled 'worry time' of 15 minutes duration - no more, no less. She may find this difficult so, for the scheduled time, you can do some enjoyed and shared activity. She may need time to trust you with her worries. Reassure her merely by allocating that time and attention. Don't be tempted into solving her problems - just share them for the time being. Help her only to describe them. Find out her feelings and thoughts regarding her school placement.

The tantrumming spontaneously remitted. After three months, I invited Chloe's parents to write about their experiences:
Dear David,

When we came to see you last year, we were all at our wits' end because of Chloe's dreadful temper tantrums and violent reactions. Prior to seeing you, we truly believed we had a severely disturbed thirteen-year-old on our terrified hands. In a relatively short time she had changed from a spirited, happy child, to what seemed to us an uncontrollable delinquent.

Our session with you has caused a complete change. The day in your office about three months ago was traumatic to all of us. We were all scared of the 'unknown' I guess. Chloe was sullen and completely silent most of the time. We could see that she had chosen to be as unco-operative as possible and were embarrassed as no parent wants one's child to be presented to a stranger at her worst. However, even though the interview opened a new can of worms and brought out a few hidden worries, we, the untrained parents, really could not see that one session with you could possibly bring about any real results. How wrong we were!

Chloe has not thrown a tantrum since then. Sure, she gets angry and frustrated at times: we all do. However, she now keeps her anger under control and disappears into her bedroom to 'let off steam'. She was very embarrassed at her trip to the Leslie Centre and to you and for being shown for the immature and childish person she was. She, within hours of leaving you, started to act in a much more responsible manner and has gone from strength to strength ever since. If only Dr Jekyll had someone like you, Mr Hyde could have slept nights!

We never got a chance to try your Temper Tantrum Control Programme. Chloe has now started her new college (the one she was so worried about) and has made friends in her first few minutes there. She appears very happy with her main worry being if she will ever find a boyfriend.

The two things which amaze us most of all this are:
1. The speed with which Chloe snapped out of her problem - literally as she left your office. We expected it to take months and several sessions with you.
2. The maturity and dignity, not to mention responsibility, she has acquired in the time since we all saw you.

We realise, as we are in the early teenage years with Chloe, there is still a long way to go and the problems are by no means over, but at least we can now discuss things rationally which is 90% of most teenage problems.

With many thanks and best wishes, MM
PS: Chloe wants to be a cookery teacher - could it have anything to do with pumpkin pies???

DECONSTRUCTION OF THE PROBLEM

Scientific and therapeutic psychologies have infiltrated many 'folk' psychologies. This is especially the case with those 'folk' psychologies that relate to childrearing. Some of the psychotherapies have singled out anger as inviolate and have confirmed the overt expression of anger as representative of psychological grace.

In the current vogue of 'self-expression' and 'ventilationism', it is virtually anger which receives central if not exclusive attention. Pent-up anger is said to poison the personality, and thus should be 'let out'. But we hear few such exhortations to honesty concerning the far more poisonous emotions of envy and resentment. (Solomon 1976)

Accordingly, temper tantrumming is often mistakenly regarded by family members, and by some therapies, as a cathartic purgation or at least as evidence of the volume of anger within the young person. Parents are often restrained from taking any effective action by their concern for not suppressing their children's feelings.

Anger can be conceptualised as an attribute of the person, a force within. Families presume different grounds for this: genetic, family dispositional, developmental, or characterological. If the problem is construed on the basis of genetic or temperamental 'theories', then one has little choice but to accommodate to the problem and make the best of a bad lot. If it is construed as developmental in nature, then one can only hope s/he grows out of it - the sooner the better. If it is construed as characterological, then s/he ought to be discouraged from repressing his/her anger for fear of psychological side-effects. All of these constructions can be very restraining in attempting to deal with the problems that relate to temper tantrums.

If the problem can be reconstructed through its externalization, presumably some of the existing pre-suppositions are indirectly undermined in the process. Also, many of these restraining beliefs can be directly deconstructed by the introduction of a distinction around anger and tantrumming. Anger can be legitimated and validated at the same time as the therapist can contend that a person must learn how, when, and where, it might be appropriately expressed. Temper tantrumming is evaluated as inappropriate to this task and instead regarded as leading to control over others and, at the same time, to losing control over one's relationship with oneself. Another way of putting this is for the therapist to express admiration for the young person's sensitivity to their own desires and wishes, but to state a concern for the insensitivity of the young person to their parents' desires and wishes.[13]

Parents are reassured that the 'programme' is not intended to turn people into 'feelingless zombies', but rather to lead them into a more satisfactory and satisfying form of emotional expression. Temper tantrummers are promised that they will feel relieved when released from the terrible yoke of their tantrums. Parents are also reassured that the deterioration in their relationship with their son or daughter can be repaired, and that they can expect to experience more 'closeness' in this relationship in the future.

To challenge the notion that anger is inherent in the person rather than something that is expressed in interpersonal context, I sometimes quote from Aristotle:

Anyone can become angry, that is easy; but to be angry with the right person and to the right degree, and at the right time, and for the right purpose, and in the right way - that is not within everybody's power and is not easy.

Or:

It is clear that anger is neither 'good' nor a 'bad' emotion, neither 'positive' nor 'negative', but depends, in any particular case, upon the circumstances and the individual, the nature of the 'offence' and its background.
(Solomon 1976)

In deconstructing the problem, it is also extremely useful to bring forth what I call 'cross-contextual contradictions'. Questions such as: "Why do you think your temper doesn't make a fool of you at school? How is it that his/her temper has no hold over him/her when on the sports field/in the gym, etc? Are you as curious as I am that you prevail over your temper when you are in the company of people your own age?" can be asked sympathetically and with genuine curiosity. In addition to providing information about problem-free contexts, these questions undermine those beliefs that cannot account for conduct varying over time and context, and provide evidence that, in many contexts, anger can be controlled and the young person is not invariably its victim.

Such deconstruction plays the role of the 'countervoice' advocated by La Perriere:

It is interesting that now we go the reverse path, and that which has been defined as incapacity or illness benefits by being defined as bad, naughty or resistive. Perhaps this suggests that therapy is a polymorphous societal invention. It becomes the countervoice to whatever is in excess in mainstream culture. (1982, p.91)

RAISING THE DILEMMA:
In control or under control?

A dilemma is raised around the stark and dramatic opposition of personal agency and passivity (self in control versus self under control). Such contrasting descriptions of the young person's relationship to the problem bring the question of responsibility into view. The tantrummer and other family members are then invited to consider his/her involvement with tantrums as a matter of choice rather than of necessity. Metaphors of being in control and under control are set in opposition to each other, and frame questions that are posed to the tantrummers and others.

The following provide some examples of such metaphors and questions:[14]

- *Are you going to get (back) into the driver's seat of your life, or are you going to permit your temper to drive you where it will?*
- *Are you going to be boss over your temper, or will it boss you around and finally push you into a corner?*
- *Are you going to be your temper's robot, or are you going to take your feelings into your own hands?*
- *Are you going to be intoxicated by tantrumming, or are you going to break away from the habit?*
- *Are you going to be duped by your temper, or are you going to give it a taste of its own medicine?*
- *Are you going to defeat and weaken your temper, or is it going to keep up its winning streak and further weaken you?*
- *Are you going to surrender more of yourself to it, or are you going to get your own back at its expense?*
- *Are you going to be ruled by your temper, or are you going to recapture yourself from its hold over you?*
- *Is your temper going to predominate over you, or will you put it in its place in your life?*

These are challenging questions and usually provoke agentic responses. These questions can be revised for other family members as well:
- *Are you going to surrender further to his/her temper's tyranny, or are you going to regain some ground, ground that is historically yours?*
- *Do you think she should get into the driver's seat in her life, or should she*

Temper Tantrum Parties

abandon herself totally into her temper's grasp?

THE USUAL ELEMENTS OF THE INTERVENTION

To sustain the intensity and interest required to present the regular elements of the intervention, intrigue is introduced. This arouses curiosity and reduces the possibility of an outbreak of tantrumming in the session. It is often helpful to ask timely questions that will appear irrelevant or, at best, tangential until the intervention is fully unveiled.

From the outset of crafting the intervention, I always attempt to secure the temper tantrummer's co-operation. I will often forecast success and form a partnership with the tantrummer on that basis:

DE: *Are you any good at writing?*

Mark: (aged 13 years) *Not bad ...*

DE: *Well, look. I'm writing a chapter on temper tantrums and a lot of the other younger people who have <u>done it</u> really couldn't figure out how they <u>did it</u>. Would you mind keeping a good record of how you <u>do it</u> and, after your tantrum-free month, I'd be willing to pay you to come back and make a videotape <u>with me</u>, telling other young people who haven't yet learned how to control their temper, <u>how you did it</u>. You'll be a consultant here. How much do you charge for your services? But you know, your writing doesn't have to have all the commas and things in place. I can <u>help you</u> with that. <u>We'll do it together</u>.*

Mark: *Is that alright, Mum? Can I do it?*

Here, co-operation is predicted on the existence of an imminent solution that the young person may both enact and discover. By the careful use of verbal tense, the therapist can consign the problem to the past. A new relationship between the young person and the problem can then be implied.

At an appropriate time after the problem has been both reconstructed and deconstructed, and after the tantrummer and his/her family are committed, at least in principle, to the 'simplicity of the solution', I put our engagement to the test:

DE: *Look, I think I can give you a money-back guarantee on the programme. If you've failed, you would be the third out of ... (current number of families) I've worked with. I don't see any reason why you'd want to fail but, if you do, I'm on the side of your success. You could lead*

Experience, Contradiction, Narrative & Imagination

a solution lifestyle rather than a problem lifestyle. But you're going to need to trust me and, within reason, I would be willing to submit myself to your testing my trustworthiness. Do you want to test me?

A willingness on the therapist's behalf to undergo testing by others seems sufficient as a test of engagement. As yet, no-one has taken this opportunity to submit me to a trustworthiness test. However, in the event of a 'yes', I would not proceed further until this matter was settled to the satisfaction of family members. Such a trustworthiness test would include family members calling up ex-clients, ex-tantrummers, colleagues, etc. in order for them to assess my competence. When family members say 'no' to the offer of putting me to the test, I involve them in some ritual of engagement - usually a solemn handshake during which the young person invites my participation in assisting them with their problem, during which I assume responsibility for the 'temper tantrum control programme', on the condition that "once begun, you must go through with it". The family can also be canvassed for support of the therapist's involvement and, if wholehearted agreement is secured, this can be sealed with handshaking all round. I will query anyone's commitment in relation to handshakes that are not firm. If the young person refuses to shake hands, I question his/her readiness to tackle the problem, but not their ability to do so - "I know you're able, but are you ready?" I then would return to a more detailed discussion of the consequences for them and their family if the problem's influence over them were to increase and family relationships were to deteriorate further. I would then schedule another meeting to review their readiness for the intervention.

The Temper Tantrum Party requires a name and guest list. The potential guests are drawn from the problem-free context which have been ascertained well in advance. Because of the social influence adolescents have over their peers, I most commonly use 'your three best friends'. Guest lists have included the Olympic coach and three Olympians in the sport of a tantrumming Olympic hopeful, team mates, Boy Scout troupe, colleagues, boy/girl friends, etc. I also enquire if these partygoers are known to the family. This is almost always the case; if not, I would ask for their addresses. The party is named according to the tantrummer's food preference:

DE: (to Mark, aged 13) *Tell me something ... what would you prefer at a party - sweet or savoury things? What would be your first choice?*

Mark: (confused) *Savoury ... don't like sweets much. Ah ... a little bit.*
DE: *Gee, a 13-year-old who doesn't have a sweet tooth.* (referring question to his mother) *This is pretty unusual!*
Mother: *No, that's right. He doesn't eat much sweets.*
DE: *Well, look ... if you went to a party and could only have one thing, what would it be?*
Mark: *A sweet.*
DE: *What kind of sweet?*
Mark: (ponders) *A chocolate log.*
DE: *Can your mother bake a chocolate log?*
Mark: *Yeah ... she's good at baking.*
DE: *Chocolate log it is!*

Parents are then provided with instructions regarding the 'cards' which are reiterated by letter.[15] This is followed at once by the 'letters of invitation'. I compose a sample letter in everyone's presence and this stands as the *denouement* of the intervention. The temper tantrummer is often shocked into silence, whereas the family is quicker to appreciate the joke. The tantrummer often regains his/her equilibrium by expostulating: "I'll just stop!" It is now that the joke is shared all around. I rapidly reassure all concerned that "there's never been a party yet and, if there is, I'll come along and bring a banana cake".

The following is a 'letter of invitation' composed for Mark, aged 13 years, who, prior to the intervention, had been tantrumming between 10 and 20 times per day:

Dear Malcolm/Steven/Graham,[16]

I would like to invite you to a Chocolate Log and Temper Tantrum Party at my house on ... (date) at ... (time). My mother and I believe that only you can help me overcome a serious problem I've got in not being able to control my anger. I know that temper tantrums are babyish. When I am with you, I act my age. I think you will be able to help me by listening to or looking at my tantrums. I will be disappointed if you can't come.   Your friend, Mark.

Sample letters such as the above are furnished with the following instructions:

Mrs H,

You are to see to it that the letters are to be written <u>in advance</u> and signed.

I argue that if the young person refuses to do so, parents should write them on their behalf. However, I contend that it would be very convincing evidence of the temper tantrummer's maturity or growing up if s/he did it unaided. I have found on reviewing cases that the struggle to procure the letters appears to have been a turning point in a minority of cases:

Mrs H,

You are to hold these addressed letters in a safe place and see to it that they are delivered when and if the time comes.

Some consideration should be given to the person selected to undertake this putative task. I often choose younger siblings or girl/boy friends.

CONSULTING YOUR CONSULTANT[17]

I customarily use a tantrum-free month as my criterion for success, although I have reduced it on occasions for particularly volatile and explosive young people. Roles are reversed in every way possible, but most significantly in regard to the matter of fees. Since s/he now holds the 'solution', payment is offered by the agency to the young person. It has always been declined, either by the young person or by their family. The session is videotaped or, failing that, audiotaped. The tantrummer is awarded the new status of 'veteran of the problem' and 'consultant to other young people regarding the solution to the problem'. Every opportunity is taken to contribute to the endurance of change and to excavate with the young person and their family his/her and their new knowledge. In other words, one of the avowed intentions is to discover their discoveries. New audiences are found so that the changes observed can be marked and ratified in a context wider than the therapist-family system. By risking the loss of face, the tantrummers not only save face but, in addition, find themselves regraded (Epston 1984). They are also more than willing to contribute written documents in the form of letters of advice to other young people, or to offer telephone consultations.

In those cases where the tantrumming is merely substantially reduced, the same procedure is followed with the additional purpose of expanding and elaborating the young person's knowledge. *You've now gone 60% of the way. Knowing what you now know will very likely take you over the finish line.* I have found that the mopping-up operation is usually not too difficult as the 'reign of terror' is now over and all parties to the problem can participate with it differently.

The following are excerpts from a 'consulting your consultant' session, seven weeks after the first meeting. Simon, aged 12 years, had tantrummed on the average of seven times per week and had assaulted his twin 15 year old sisters. His single parent mother had been reluctant to leave their home for fear that there would be violence between Simon and his sisters. Simon had retreated into his own room, whereas the other family members moved fearfully around the house.

I take pains to honour this young man in particular and the other family members in general. I also attend to the individual family members' responses to his victory against temper and their defeat of fear. If, as in this family, there have been many changes in many parts of the family system - for example, Simon's new claim to honesty, his mother's willingness to insist on his equal participation in the household and its daily activities, the commencement of the repair of the sibling relationships, and Simon's newfound co-operation - then I raise the question with the family whether they wish to meet again "over anything". In a minority of cases, the family and I have embarked upon new initiatives on further matters of their concern.

The Preamble

DE: *Simon, it seemed to me that you had been driven into a life of irresponsibility by your temper. It had gotten the better of you and was making you look immature and silly. Then you decided, along with your mother and your sisters, that you didn't want to be victims of this any longer. And you were, in fact, its biggest victim, although they too were being victimized by your temper taking you over and taking them over. It seemed to me that you were feeling that everyone else was quite close together and you were being pushed away.*

The Review

DE: *Well, what happened to the temper tantrumming Nicola?*
Nicola: *He's been given the first card and then he just kinda stopped. He's been really good though.*
DE: *Have you been finding that you are having a better brother and sister relationship?*

Experience, Contradiction, Narrative & Imagination

Nicola: *Yes.*

Mother: *I've been amazed! I can show him the first card. Admittedly, you sat there once and tore it into pieces. Then you got the second card. I think he might have actually got to the final warning. That was only once that happened ... it was near the beginning. But generally since then, occasionally the card gets waved and that's all he needs.*

Discovering their Discoveries

DE: *Could you explain to me how you did this work on yourself? How you did this work on your temper? What did you do?*

Simon: *I didn't want to be embarrassed by Mum handing out those things to my friends.*

DE: *Yeah, I know you wouldn't. A lot of people wouldn't want to be embarrassed by something like that, but they don't do anything about it ... they really can't do anything about their problem ... you did. How did you do that bit?*

Simon: *Well ... I just ... I was getting further away from my family ... so, whenever I was shown a card I tried to fight it.*

DE: *Did that thought give you strength to get the better of your temper?*

Simon: *Yeah.*

DE: *Really ... I guess your family gives you a lot of strength? And you give them a lot of strength?*

Simon: *Yeah.*

DE: *That's what families are for - to strengthen one another. Do you think that your sisters have stopped being afraid of you, or are they taking a little while to get their courage back?*

Simon: *They are better.*

DE: *How are they better? How are they improved?*

Simon: *They do things for me ... like I asked my sister to make breakfast for me and she did.*

DE: *And before, what would have happened?*

Simon: *She would have usually said "no" or "get it yourself".*

DE: *Why do you think she is more giving to you now?*

Simon: *Because I am more pleasant.*

DE: (to mother) *Have you noticed him being more pleasant?*

Mother: *Yes ... yes!*

Temper Tantrum Parties

DE: *What's it like?*

Mother: (laughing) *Quite nice.*

DE: *Can I ask: Remember how things used to be when he was having 7 tantrums a week? What percentage improvement has there been in your family life since temper tantrums have been kicked out of your family?*

Mother: *Well, I'd say about 80%. There are times he still explodes on the spot but he seems to cool off quickly. The girls aren't pussy-footing around him any more. They ask him for something and he co-operates.*

DE: *I don't think this programme really stops people being angry at all. It just teaches them to get control over themselves and their feelings. Because once they start running away with you, you get put into the grip of your temper. And once you are in the grip of your temper, it's like being in the grip of intoxicating liquor. You get drunk on it and don't know what you are doing. So the girls aren't pussy-footing around him any more? What about yourself?*

Mother: *Well, I find I ask him to do things and eventually he does them - sometimes straight off. I'm not avoiding asking him any more because of a temper tantrum. I'll nag now until he does it.*

DE: *Well, he's inviting your nagging.*

.....

DE: *Are you surprised how strong and big you were when you really started going against your temper? And how you could make such short work of it?*

Simon: *Yeah.*

DE: *How long did you think it would take you before you would control your temper?*

Simon: *Ages!*

DE: *How long did you think it would take? Did you think he would be about 30 before he ever would?*

Nicola: *I thought it would take quite a while.*

DE: *How many years, months, weeks, or days?*

Nicola: *About six months.*

Mother: *About twelve months.*

DE: *That's what most people say. You must be pretty surprised. He's a real hero to get the better of it so quickly.*

Mother: *I was quite surprised ... It's made him take control of himself without me having to do very much. He had to stop and think. And just generally it's made a difference in him. He's nicer to have around.*

DE: *He's a victor; he's nicer to have around. Any other ways you've noticed him being a bigger and better person?*

Mother: *Well, he went through a stage of taking money out of my bag. He actually said to me: "Do you realise I haven't done it for ages and I'm not going to do it any more!"*

DE: *He's also got control over his dishonesty.*

Mother: *Yes.*

DE: *Any other signs that he's done a leap in his growing up?*

Mother: *Generally he's doing things ... he's more co-operative around the place.*

.....

DE: *Are you ready for a bigger dose of responsibility? You're only 12 and a half. Can you take the pressure of it? Can you take it?*

Simon: *Yeah!*

DE: *If your mother started giving you more responsibility, could you stand up to it or would you crack?*

Simon: *I could bear to stand up to it.*

DE: *If you could stand up to your tantrums, I figure you could stand up to more responsibility.*

.....

DE: *Do you think he's nicer to you?*

Nicola: *Yeah.*

DE: *In what way do you see him being nicer?*

Nicola: *I don't know. Just before he wouldn't talk to you at all. He'd go into his bedroom and stay there.*

DE: *Wow! He was getting a long way away from his family, wasn't he?*

Nicola: *Yeah.*

DE: *Is he coming out of his room more?*

Nicola: *Yeah, but sometimes he goes into his room to kinda calm down a bit.*

DE: *Oh, what a good idea! Did you figure that out?*

Simon: *I don't know.*

DE: *That's a pretty good idea. Well, you don't frighten people when you are in your room.*

Nicola: *Sometimes he goes into his room and sits down for a while and pats the dog. And then comes out ...*

Temper Tantrum Parties

DE: *What an excellent idea! Hold on ... Maybe this is what you've been doing instead of going off your face and looking silly. You go into your room where you are on your own and no-one can see you and get angry and pat the dog and get over it. Talk to the dog and tell it how mean your mother is and your sisters are terrible. And I bet that dog understands you and you feel a bit better. Did you invent this idea of going into your room and patting the dog, or did you get some advice on it?*
Simon: *No ... I just go in and pat the dog.*
DE: *You made it up? This is quite a good invention ... A good discovery. Did you know that you had discovered this?*
Simon: *No.*
DE: *Are you making a discovery that you have made a discovery?*
Simon: *No.*
DE: *So, right now, you've making a discovery that you have made a discovery?*
Simon: *No.*
DE: *Well, am I getting through to you what a good idea this is? What a good discovery?*
Simon: *Yes.*
DE: *Am I getting through to you?*
Simon: *Yes.*
DE: *Do you think I've got it through to you?*
Simon: *Yes.*
DE: *Well, when you came here today, you didn't even know you had made this invention?*
Simon: *No.*
DE: *But you noticed he had been going into his room and cooling down instead of going off his head?*
Nicola: *Mmh.*
DE: *That's very good. Would you recommend that to other young men or women?*
Simon: *Yeah!*
DE: *It's a good idea!*
Simon: *It'd be a bit bad if they didn't have a dog.*
DE: *A cat, teddy bear, or even a punching bag. How did you come to that discovery?*
Simon: *I don't know.*

Experience, Contradiction, Narrative & Imagination

DE: *What made you do it - go in there, cool down, pat the dog, be a bit grumpy and then come out and be a nice person? What made you do it?*
Simon: *I didn't want to get a card ... because no-one can usually see me.*
DE: (to mother) *Did you know he was doing this?*
Mother: *Well, now that Nicola brought it up, I did. I show him a card and quite often he takes himself off to his room.*
DE: *He's getting in control.*
Mother: *Yes, he did.*
DE: *Did you decide to go to your room and wrestle with your temper? Is that why you went there to win over it without anyone looking?*
Simon: *Yeah.*
DE: *When no-one was looking, did that help you win over it?*
Simon: *Yeah.*
DE: *Did you think you would have a better chance to win with people looking or being on your own?*
Simon: *A bit of both really!*
DE: *How's that?*
Simon: *Well, sometimes I do it when they're all around and sometimes I go into my room.*
DE *So you've got two ways of beating it.*
Simon: *Yeah.*
DE: *Sometimes out in the open, and sometimes behind closed doors.*
Simon: *Yeah!*

SURVEY OF OUTCOMES

Family therapy practitioners have often been criticized for their unwillingness to evaluate their outcomes (see Humphreys 1980; Cross 1982). There has never been a strong adherence to the rigorous application of controlled group studies for both epistemological and practical reasons. Despite the more obvious utility of single case methodologies, such research designs have not come into favour (see Cross 1984). On the other hand, there has been a call for outcome studies undertaken by practitioners, unburdened by the requirements of methodological 'robustness'. The evidence is then 'soft' but the argument is carried on the basis of large samples with statistically significant results. This survey is well placed within this tradition although, admittedly, rough-and-ready.

The following questionnaire was forwarded to as many family therapists as I knew who had used at least some of the constant elements of the 'temper tantrum party' approach to out-of-control behaviours.

Temper Tantrum Party Questionnaire

1. How many times do you estimate you have used some of the constant elements of the Temper Tantrum Party approach to anger control problems?
2. What were the ages of the temper tantrummers? Or, what do you estimate was the average age of your population of temper tantrummers?
3. The temper tantrumming itself:
   never occurred again;
   dramatically diminished;
   substantially diminished;
   diminished;
   no change;
   increased.
4. Did you use a prescribed period of time for follow-up? If so, specify in weeks, months, or years what that time was.
5. How many meetings were required to get the result noted in Question 3? In each case, or on the average, if you have a large sample.
6. Please detail your reasons for either failure of the 'programme' or its withdrawal.
7. Please detail the most violent or assaultive young person you have successfully dealt with through the constant elements of the temper tantrum party approach.
8. Under what circumstances would you not apply such an approach?
9. Any other comments you would like to make about the temper tantrum party approach to anger control problems?
10. Do you have any objections to your name, profession, or work place being cited?

I received fourteen written replies and one verbal report. I have included my own results to make the number up to sixteen. The respondents worked in a wide variety of settings (child psychiatry, residential programmes, community mental health centres, and private practices), although they all were child and family-centred. The outcomes reported then are trans-Tasman, cross-therapist, and cross-agency.

The number of individuals affected by the intervention was 131, with a mean of 8.19 per respondent (range 1-36). I had been required to replace 'families' or 'cases' with individuals as there were several cases with more than one tantrumming family member. The maximum was five family members within one family. Almost all the information was derived from six-month follow-ups, with a reasonable number of one-year follow-ups. Almost all reported an average of 2-3 sessions, with a range of 1-5.

The following is a range of comment to questions 6-8:

The poor results were all in situations where, for one reason or another, I did not manage to get the parents hooked on the idea and committed to an active approach, e.g. in one case, the parents were planning their separation and this became their main preoccupation. In another case, the parents did not think there was a problem, although the school did. (Kerry Callaghan, Genesis Centre, Whangarei, NZ)

I would not use such an approach with children who have an uncertain place in their family or with families in which the parents used powerful forms of punishment, e.g. parents were tyrannical rather than the child. (Gay Bayfield, Leslie Centre, Auckland, NZ)

I suspect there are situations in which I wouldn't use it. I've found it most useful in cases of identifiable or episodic outbursts, rather than in cases of more generalised, more constant behaviour problems. In some ways, the more violent the kid, the better it works - so I wouldn't waste it on a kid whose violence was not convincing enough. I have had a number of parents who initially baulked at it and are concerned that it is unfair, blackmail, or will damage Johnny's self-esteem. This is a useful reflection of their belief systems. I usually manage to overcome this minor hurdle with a laugh and a comment about damaging his self-esteem versus continuing to have their heads damaged, but it could fluster some therapists. (Michael Durrant, Eastwood Family Therapy Centre, Sydney, Australia)

Others pointed out the failure to gain the co-operation of the tantrummer. Kerry Callaghan and Laurie Hinchcliff (Glenburn Centre, Auckland, NZ) cautioned against its use with rigid families or in families where there is profound marital discord.

The following is a sample of responses to Question 7:

1. A fourteen year old Maori young man who used to attack his mother with a carving knife. She believed him to be taken over by one of his ancestors.

The suggestion of time out and a Temper Tantrum Party involving his tribal elders resulted in his mother taking charge of him. The young man subsequently decided to join a Maori culture group so that he could learn traditional Maori challenges. His temper tantrums were dramatically reduced and his family now manages him better and feel safe to walk off and ignore him if he looks like he is going to get into one of his rages. (Kerry Callaghan)

2. *A twelve year old boy described in the first interview as "violent, frequently hurts two younger brothers, hits mother. Throws things, makes threats including running away and killing himself. Relations can't stand him. Throws tantrums if annoyed and can't fight without becoming hysterical. Describes himself as out of control." (Gay Bayfield)*

3. *A young man, aged 16-17, spoke incessantly of murduring his mother and had taken a gun to school and shot holes in the roof. Both the therapists and family were concerned that he would kill his mother. On follow-up, they were all very happy and he had left school and obtained a job. (Simon Kennedy, Melbourne)*

The results are extremely impressive:

		%age
Never occurred again:	60	45
Dramatically diminished:	56	42
Substantially diminished:	10	8
Diminished:	2	2
No change:	2	2
Increased:	1	1
Total:	131	100

The high percentage of clustering in the 'never occurred again' and 'dramatically reduced' categories (116 = 87%) is a convincing argument for the effectiveness of the intervention. The 'never occurred again' category might even have been higher if the parents had been asked to discriminate carefully between 'tantrumming' and 'anger' and its appropriate expression. I have known some parents to report tantrumming for any expression of anger, even that occurring within the time limits of the intervention. A more careful discussion can lead to the young person appreciating their

Experience, Contradiction, Narrative & Imagination

self-interventions and their parents acknowledging them for it. The average of 2-3 sessions argues for its economy as, previously, many of these young people would have been admitted to long-term residential programmes or psychiatric treatment - much of which must be considered as custodial or containment. Such services are notoriously expensive and hard to run.

I believe that the intervention preserves the dignity of these young people and the integrity of their families. Many other families with whom I have utilized this intervention were on the point of exiling the tantrummer, or another of the family members - usually the mother - was considering self-exile. Either way, many of these families, on referral, were escalating towards breakdown. Also, I have found that many such families, once they have decided to take action, are willing to accept nothing short of a dramatic reduction in tantrumming before they will consider any intervention a success. Often, reports of diminished or substantially diminished incidents are regarded by these families as insufficient; they are so terrorised as to deem such improvements as merely a reprieve and nothing more. For these reasons, results must be extraordinarily dramatic if they are to go over the tantrummer's and family's threshold for 'news of difference' that relationships are and can be different. Many parents report similar remarks to John Boylan:

I think we're still in shock over it ... it's all been too easy. When we talk about it now, it makes it sound as if it wasn't so bad. But I've never met anyone like it (referring to 9-year-old daughter).

The fact that the intervention is almost always experienced by all concerned as a joke is extremely helpful. On review, all the families I have worked with had begun repairing their deteriorated relationships and the parents had rapidly re-assumed their parenting entitlement. All the ex-tantrummers have reported a great relief, feeling more in control of their feelings and the course of their lives, and a good deal of satisfaction with their family reunion. I have also used variations of this intervention, employing different contexts of ideas, with men who are violent to their partners and children. Although the number is very small by comparison, the results are as favourable.[18]

I have used this intervention 36 times over a 9 year period and, with practice, the proportion of 'never occurred again' to 'dramatically reduced' is increasing to the extent that I now offer 'double your money back' guarantees to families. I have no hesitation in recommending this intervention.

Several young people have commented: *What makes you think you are good at your job? I could have figured that out myself!* I agree wholeheartedly with them. It is interesting to speculate why such interventions haven't emerged before 1979.[19] I am encouraged by the arrival of the constructivist approach to emotion, an approach that is both language-based and contextual. This work holds considerable promise in making sense of such clinical practices as outlined above (see Averill 1980; Sabini & Silver 1982; and Harre 1986).

NOTES

1. "Going off your face" is an Australian colloquialism for temper tantrumming.

2. This occurred in 1979. Versions of this paper have been presented at the New Zealand Family Therapy Conference (1983) and the Australian Family Therapy Conference (1986).

3. All names are fictitious.

4. A theoretical discussion will be available in a forthcoming paper. Any such discussion would start from Goffman's work on facework and embarrassment (Goffman 1956, 1959, 1963 & 1967). The most recent summary would be Silver, Sabini and Parrott, 1988.

5. 40 (30%) of the 131 interventions reported in the outcome study were undertaken in two Sydney residential care programmes (Burnside and Care Force - Michael Durrant, Eastwood Family Therapy Centre, consulted to both these programmes.) All involved adolescents who were either in residential care, or whose parents had approached those agencies for residential care. The violence of these adolescents were described as "assaultive of parents, family and neighbours, smashing property, 2-4 hour long tantrums, biting, and making 'animal' noises".

6. This article should be read alongside White's "Ritual of Inclusion" (1986). I prefer to reserve the 'ritual of inclusion' for those young people who have not experienced any sustained sense of 'belonging', and for those adults in their lives who have not been able to 'belong' them.

7. See White (1988) for examples of direct and indirect questions. Compare: "How did you manage to take this step?" as an example of a direct question, to: "What do you think this achievement, as a signpost, tells me about the nature of your new direction?" as an example of an indirect question.

8. See Caplan & Hall-McCorquodale (1985a, 1985b) for a critique of mother-blaming in the major clinical journals relating to children and family problems.

9. 'Gaslighting' is used as a metaphor - drawn from the classic film "Gaslight" in which a husband (played by Charles Boyer) attempts to drive his wife (played by Ingrid Bergman) mad by systematically altering the grounds of her reality - by Gass & Nichols (1988), to describe how unfaithful husbands try to convince their suspicious wives they are imagining things. Some of the more able young people reported in this paper have also been 'gaslighting' their parents in a similar fashion. They often convince their parents that they have merely imagined making requests and that, in fact, they haven't.

10. It was noted above that, while it is objectively possible to draw a distinction between the body and the world, such a distinction is much more blurred and problematic in a behavioural environment. Thus any conceptual system must embody such a distinction, even though where that distinction will be drawn is not given **a priori**. That is, a fundamental dimension in any conceptual system - and hence in the domain of control - is between those things that are held to be intrinsic to the conceiver, and those things that are intrinsic (Lock 1981, p.28-29).

11. Eileen Swann, Family Therapist, Leslie Centre.

12. White 1983 (May), workshop held at the Leslie Centre, Auckland, New Zealand.

13. This frame of reference has been applied with success to temper tantrumming and extreme non-compliance in pre-schoolers in a project undertaken with Donna Hourigan-Johnson and Jan Rodwell at Leslie Centre (1988). Parents are invited to consider, via complementary questioning, balancing their children's self-sensivity and other (parent)-insensitivity **and** their sensitivity to others (children) and their insensitivity to self, especially in the case of mothers. This will be the subject of a forthcoming publication.

14. The following questions are merely slight modifications of some wellknown dilemma questions invented by Michael White and presented in workshops in New Zealand and Australia in the period 1982-6. See also Epston, D. & White, M. "Consulting Your Consultants' Consultants", 1985.

15. Refer to the Temper Tantrum Control Programme, A & B, in this article.

16. Mark's three best friends.

17. See Epston & White 1989a.

18. This approach with modifications has been used by Kennedy (1987) for persistent sibling disputes, and by Esler (1988) for a young woman diagnosed as manic-depressive.

19. Reading the literature, I did locate some clinical reports, similar to my own, made some time ago in a residential community for delinquent and violent youth:
"One of the greatest surprises during the many baffling experiences at Pioneer House was the discovery that, after a certain amount of total ego improvement, even the most severe and obviously extremely pathological temper tantrums of a specific child could be avoided by a well-timed attempt at ... kidding the youngster out of it ... The reason why a skilled approach by the technique of ... tension decontamination ... would work and the conditions under which the effect is secured are still a puzzle to us." (Redl & Wineman 1957, p.415)
Despite several intrapsychic speculations, nothing could satisfactorily fit these chance discoveries and they were lost.

ACKNOWLEDGEMENTS

This paper has been made possible by the encouragement and editorial assistance of Ann Epston, Fred Seymour, John Kaye, and Michael White.

REFERENCES

Averill, J.R. 1980:
A constructivist view of emotion. In Plutchik, R. & Ketterman, H. (Eds.) **Emotion: Theory, research and experience, Vol.1, Theories of Emotion**.
Caplan, P.J. & Hall-McCorquodale, I. 1985:
Mother-blaming in major clinical journals. **American Journal of Orthopsychiatry**, 55:3.
Caplan, P.J. & Hall-McCorquodale, I. 1985:
The scape-goating of mothers: A call for change. **American Journal of Orthopsychiatry**, 55:4.
Cross, D. 1982:
Overview of outcome research in family therapy: Methodological considerations. **Australian Journal of Family Therapy**, 4:3.
Cross, D. 1984:
Single-case design: The neglected alternative for the evaluation of family therapy. **Australian Journal of Family Therapy**, 5:4.
Epston, D. 1984:
Guest Address, Fourth Australian Family Therapy Conference, **Australian Journal of Family Therapy**, 5(1):11-16.
Epston, D. & White, M. 1985:
Consulting your consultants' consultant.**Proceedings of the Sixth Australian Family Therapy Conference**. Melbourne; Victorian Association of Family Therapy.

Epston, D. & White, M. 1989a:
  Consulting your consultants: A documentary. Unpublished manuscript.
Epston, D. & White, M. 1989b:
  Literate Means to Therapeutic Ends. Adelaide; Dulwich Centre Publications.
Esler, I. 1988:
  Standing up to madness: Temper in disguise. Presented at **Dulwich Centre**, March.
Gass, G.Z. & Nichols, W.C. 1988:
  Gaslighting: A marital syndrome. **Contemporary Family Therapy**, 10:1.
Goffman, E. 1956:
  Embarrassment and social organisation. **American Journal of Sociology**, 62.
Goffman, E. 1959:
  The Presentation of Self in Everyday Life. Garden City, New York; Doubleday.
Goffman, E. 1963:
  Stigma. Englewood Cliffs, N.J.; Prentice Hall.
Goffman, E. 1987:
  Interaction Ritual. New York; Doubleday.
Harre, R. (Ed.) 1986:
  The Social Construction of Emotion. Oxford; Basil Blackwell.
Humphreys, J. 1980:
  Family therapy - Review of outcome research. **Australian Journal of Family Therapy**, 2:3.
Kennedy, S. 1987:
  Bickering and bikkie party. **Australian & New Zealand Journal of Family Therapy**, 8:2.
La Perriere, K. 1982:
  Heroin, my baby. **Australian Journal of Family Therapy**, 10:1.
Lock, A. 1981:
  Universals in human conception. In Heelas, P. & Lock, A. (Eds.) **Indigenous Psychologies: The anthropology of the self**. London; Academic Press.
Redl, F. & Wineman, D. 1957:
  The Aggressive Child. Glencoe, Illinois; Free Press.
Sabini, J. & Silver, M. 1982:
  Moralities of Everyday Life. Oxford; University Press.
Silver, M., Sabini, J. & Parrott, W.G. 1988:
  Embarrassment: A dramaturgical account. **Journal of the Theory of Social Behaviour**, 17:1.
Solomon, R.C. 1976:
  The Passions: The myth and nature of human emotion. Garden City, New York; Anchor Press.
Tomm, K. 1989:
  Externalizing the problem and internalizing personal agency. **Journal of Strategic & Systemic Therapies**. Accepted for publication.
Turner, B. & Hepworth, M. 1982:
  Confessions: Studies in deviance. London; Routledge & Kegan Paul.

White, M. 1984:
Pseudo-encopresis: From avalanche to victory, from vicious to virtuous cycles.**Family Systems Medicine**, 2:2. Republished in White, M., 1991,**Selected Papers**. Adelaide; Dulwich Centre Publications.

White, M. 1985:
Fear busting and monster taming.**Dulwich Centre Review**, pp.29-34. Republished in White, M., 1991, **Selected Papers**. Adelaide; Dulwich Centre Publications.

White, M. 1986a:
Ritual of inclusion: An approach to extreme uncontrolled behaviour in children and young adolescents. **Dulwich Centre Review**, pp.20-27. Republished in White, M., 1991, **Selected Papers**. Adelaide; Dulwich Centre Publications.

White, M. 1986b:
Negative explanation, restraint and double description: A template for family therapy. **Family Process**, 25:2. Republished in White, M., 1991, **Selected Papers**. Adelaide; Dulwich Centre Publications.

White, M. 1986c:
Family escape from trouble. **Case Studies**, 1:1. Republished in White, M., 1991, **Selected Papers**. Adelaide; Dulwich Centre Publications.

White, M. 1987:
Family therapy and schizophrenia: Addressing the 'in-the-corner' lifestyle.**Dulwich Centre Newsletter**, Spring, pp.14-21. Republished in White, M., 1991, **Selected Papers**. Adelaide; Dulwich Centre Publications.

White, M. 1988:
The process of questioning: A therapy of literary merit?**Dulwich Centre Newsletter**, Winter, pp.8-14. Republished in White, M., 1991,**Selected Papers**. Adelaide; Dulwich Centre Publications.

White, M. 1988/89:
The externalizing of the problem and the re-authoring of lives and relationships. **Dulwich Centre Newsletter**, Summer, pp.3-21. Republished in White, M., 1991, **Selected Papers**. Adelaide; Dulwich Centre Publications.

White, M. & Epston, D. 1989:
Literate Means to Therapeutic Ends. Adelaide; Dulwich Centre Publications. Republished as **Narrative Means to Therapeutic Ends**. New York; W.W.Norton.

CHAPTER IV

FAMILY THERAPY TRAINING AND SUPERVISION IN A WORLD OF EXPERIENCE AND NARRATIVE

Michael White

*Previously published in
Dulwich Centre Newsletter
Summer 1989/90.*

The narrative metaphor has provided for a novel interpretation of family therapy and, in so doing, has precipitated a re-evaluation of and a significant revisioning of the therapeutic process. This metaphor has enabled us to conceive of this process as one that establishes the opportunity for people to re-author their lives and their relationships according to alternative stories that have preferred outcomes. It encourages us to envision the role of therapist as co-author, and to consider what transformations in the structure of therapy might be necessary in order to render it a more effective restorying context.

The narrative metaphor also provides for a novel interpretation of training and supervision as a context for the re-authoring of stories about therapy, and of the participant's "life as therapist". Under the guidance of this metaphor, the restructuring of training and supervision invites participants into experiences that parallel the experiences of those people who are the "recipients" of family therapy.

SETTING THE STRUCTURE

The expectations of "teachers/supervisors" and "participants" about the context and structure of training and supervision are highly significant. Usually these expectations are intimately related to the ideas held by both parties about the nature of the therapeutic endeavour. Such expectations set the scene for what is to take place in training and supervision.

For example, at times the context of therapy is informed by a "positivist" view and by the idea that it is possible for "experts" to be impartial and to undertake an objective evaluation of the problems that families present for therapy; by the idea that it is both reasonable and desirable to subject families to certain evaluative procedures in order to determine an objective and assured "truth" of the problem (in terms of disorders/psychopathologies/dysfunctions etc). With such an approach, there is an attempt to reduce the complexity of observed phenomena and to remove uncertainty from the situation. Therapists are encouraged to institute measures that are corrective of the diagnosed problem; interventions designed to "get at" whatever it is that is constructed as the truth of the problem.

It could be expected that any training and supervision that is informed by these ideas would place emphasis on the participant learning the "correct" methods of evaluation, developing "precision" in diagnosis according to a system of constructed and approved "truths", and perfecting "known" and specified skills in a technology of interviewing; to subject him/herself to the teacher's/supervisor's expert knowledge. We could predict that the participant would be encouraged to evaluate, correct, regulate, and in other ways discipline him/her self in an effort to replicate and perfect the evaluative procedures and this technology of interviewing. This would be associated with a consistent effort, on behalf of the teacher/supervisor, to reduce complexity and remove uncertainty in the teaching/supervision context.

Other ideas about the nature of the therapeutic endeavour will have different implications for the structure of training and supervision. In this paper, I will present some thoughts about a structure for training and supervision that is informed by ideas derived from the "text analogy" or "narrative metaphor".

INFORMED CHOICE

If there is a considerable degree of matching of the expectations of participants and teachers/supervisors, then both parties will experience a degree of comfort with their interaction in the training/supervision context. However, such a matching is not always achieved and, although disputes that arise out of conflicting expectations can be approached in ways that are generative of some unique and positive outcomes, more often, because of the power differential, resolution occurs in favour of the expectations of the teacher/supervisor.

Because the framework of ideas is so formative of the structure of training/supervision, and because conflicts in expectations can be entirely problematic for participants and for teachers/supervisors, it is important that any decision made by therapists to enrol in training courses or to contract supervision be a decision arrived at on the basis of an informed choice. To some extent, this can be achieved if the therapist seeking training/supervision is provided with knowledge about the ideas and practices of therapy that are embraced by the teacher/supervisor, and with information about the nature and structure of the training/supervision context.

If this information is readily available, therapists will have the opportunity to determine which approach to therapy and to training/supervision fits with what they perceive to be preferred ideas, practices and values.

In the following discussion, I have endeavoured to provide an outline of some of the ideas that I believe to frame my practices of therapy and of training/supervision. My bias is for a processual analysis (the unique location of events in an irreversible and transformative march through time) rather than a structural one (the interpretation of events according to rules laid down in deep structure), and I currently prefer the text analogy or narrative metaphor for the framing of phenomena in therapy and in training/supervision.

I consider the discussion of ideas presented in this paper to be partial. I have chosen to focus here on the text analogy, while appreciating the fact that this analogy is limited in its ability to interpret particular events in social systems. For example, it does not address the broader fields of knowledge and power that people are subject to, and it does not focus on the specific techniques of power that people are incited to employ in making up their lives and relationships - those well established "practices of self" and "practices of relationship". I have discussed the text analogy in relation to general fields of power and knowledge elsewhere, as well as the specific techniques of a modern system of power (White 1988/89, 1989). In a forthcoming publication I will present some thoughts about the dominant practices of self - practices that relate to the person's construction of self and to the person's relationship with the self - in "modern" culture, and the relevance of these to therapy.

THE WORLD OF EXPERIENCE AND NARRATIVE

In the social sciences at least, it is now generally recognised that it is not possible for persons to have a direct knowledge of the world; that an objective description of the world is not available to us, and that no-one has a privileged access to the naming of reality, whatever that reality is.

And it is generally accepted that what we know of the world, we know only through our experience of it; our experience of the world is all that we have, and this is all that we can know. We cannot even know another person's experience of the world. The best that we can do is to interpret the experience of others; that is, the expressions of their experience as they go about the business of interpreting it for themselves.[1]

Whatever sense we have of how things stand with someone else's inner life, we gain it through their expressions, not through some magical intrusion into their consciousness. It's all a matter of scratching surfaces. (Geertz 1986, p.373)

And to interpret the expressions (and thus the interpretations) of others, we have to rely upon our own lived experience and imagination. The most that we can do is to "identify" our own experience of the experience as expressed by others. Thus "empathy" is a critical factor in the interpretation or understanding of the experiences of others.

So, this is all that we have - our lived experience of the world. But this turns out to be a very great deal. We are rich in lived experience. To quote Geertz (1986):

We all have very much more of the stuff than we know what to do with, and if we fail to put it into some graspable form, the fault must lie in a lack of means, not of substance. (p.373)

Certain questions are raised by any serious consideration of this proposal about the world of experience.
- Given that what we know of the world we know through our experience of it, what is the process by which we develop an understanding of our experience and give meaning to it?
- How do we make sense of our experience to ourselves, and how do we make sense of our experience to others?
- If we are perpetually involved in an attempt to articulate our lived experience to ourselves and to others, what processes are involved in our interpretation of it?
- What is it that facilitates the expression of our experience?
- And how does the expression of our lived experience affect our lives and relationships?

These questions focus our attention on an investigation of the ways that we make sense of our lives to ourselves and to others; they focus our attention on the processes through which we interpret or attribute meaning to our experience.

In order to give meaning to experience we must organize it, frame it, or give pattern to it. To understand an aspect of our experience, we must be able to frame it within a pattern of experience that is known to us; we must be able to identify aspects of lived experience within the context of known patterns of experience.

Stories or Narratives

Those social scientists whose work is oriented by the "interpretive method" and who embrace the text analogy, propose that the "story" or the "narrative" provides the dominant frame for lived experience; for the organization and patterning of lived experience (Geertz 1983; E. Bruner 1986).

Following this proposal, a story can be defined as a unit of meaning that provides a frame for lived experience. It is through these stories that lived experience is interpreted. We enter into stories, we are entered into stories by others, and we live our lives through these stories.

Stories enable persons to link aspects of their experience through the dimension of time. There does not appear to be any other mechanism for the structuring of experience that so captures the sense of lived time, or that can adequately represent the sense of lived time (Ricoeur 1983). It is through stories that we obtain a sense of our lives changing. It is through stories that we are able to gain a sense of the unfolding of the events of our lives through recent history, and it appears that this sense is vital to the perception of a "future" that is in any way different from a "present". Stories construct beginnings and endings; they impose beginnings and endings on the flow of experience.

> *We create the units of experience and meaning from the continuity of life. Every telling is an arbitrary imposition of meaning on the flow of memory, in that we highlight some causes and discount others; that is, every telling is interpretive.* (E. Bruner 1986, p.7)

In considering the vital role that stories have in relation to the organization of experience, it can be argued that:
- It is the stories in which we situate our experience that determine[2] the meaning that we give to experience.
- It is these stories that determine the selection of those aspects of experience to be expressed.
- It is these stories that determine the shape of the expression that we give to these aspects of experience.

Experience, Contradiction, Narrative & Imagination

- It is these stories that determine real effects and directions in our lives and in our relationships.

Performance as Shaping

In the foregoing discussion, I have argued that experience structures expression. But it can also be argued that expression structures experience. To quote Dilthey (1976):

Our knowledge of what is given in experience is extended through the interpretation of the objectifications of life and their interpretation, in turn, is only made possible by plumbing the depths of subjective experience. (p.195)

Thus, the stories that we enter into with our experience have real effects on our lives. The expression of our experience through these stories shapes or makes-up our lives and our relationships; our lives are shaped or constituted through the very process of the interpretation of experience within the context of the stories that we enter into and that we are entered into by others.

This is not to propose that life is synonymous with text. It is not enough for a person to tell a new story about oneself, or to assert claims about oneself. Instead, the proposition carried by these assertions about the world of experience and narrative is that life is the performance[3] of texts. And it is the performance of these texts that is transformative of persons' lives.

... the participants must have confidence in their own authenticity, which is one reason cultures are performed. It is not enough to assert claims; they must be enacted. Stories become transformative only in their performance. (E. Bruner 1986, p.25)

Thus, the idea that lives are situated in texts or stories implies a particular notion of authenticity - that a person arrives at a sense of authenticity in life through the performance of texts. This notion of authenticity may be affronting to many a cherished belief that carries propositions about the "truth" of personhood or of human nature; those beliefs that suggest that, under particular and ideal circumstances of life, persons will be "released" and thus become truly who they are - authentic!

Indeterminate Nature of Stories

If persons' lives are shaped through the storying of experience and through the performance of these stories, and if there is a limited stock of familial stories about who we might be and of cultural knowledges about personhood, how is it that we are not replicas of each other?

Perhaps this question is best approached by considering the interaction of readers and literary texts. To do so would be to extend the text analogy in our attempts to more fully understand the processes involved in the ascription of meaning, and to liken life as lived under the guidance of stories to the reader's experience under the sway of the literary text. And since good stories are more transformative of the reader's experience than poor stories, this consideration could bring us to a review of the structure of texts of literary merit.

In following this premise, I believe that Iser, a literary theorist, assists us to find an answer to the question, "How is it that we are not replicas of each other?"

... fictional texts constitute their own objects and do not copy something already in existence. For this reason they cannot have the full determinacy of real objects, and indeed, it is the element of indeterminacy that evokes the text to "communicate" with the reader, in the sense that they induce him to participate both in the production and the comprehension of this work's intention. (1978, p.21)

It is readily apparent that all stories are indeterminate.[4] There is a degree of ambiguity and uncertainty to all stories and, as well, there are inconsistencies and contradictions. This fact will be appreciated by those who have read a novel that was particularly engaging and then gone to a movie of the same novel, only to find, to their dismay, that the movie director got it wrong! In such a circumstance, what is clear is that the director arrived at a different interpretation of the story through his/her unique negotiation of its indeterminacy.

So, literary texts are full of gaps that readers must fill in order for the story to be performed.[5] And, in likening the interaction of readers and literary texts to the interaction of persons and the stories they live their lives through, just as these gaps in literary texts recruit the lived experience and the imagination of the reader, so do the gaps in the stories that are "lived by" recruit the lived experience and the imagination of people as they

Experience, Contradiction, Narrative & Imagination

engage in performances of meaning under the guidance of the story.

Thus, with every performance, persons are re-authoring their lives and their relationships. And every telling encapsulates, but is more than the previous telling. The evolution of the lives and relationships of persons is akin to the process of re-authoring, the process of persons entering into stories with their experience and their imagination, of taking these stories over and of making them their own.

The indeterminacy of texts and the constitutive aspect of the performance of texts provide good cause to celebrate. Clifford Geertz quotes Lionel Trilling, who is in turn quoting an eighteenth-century aesthetician's lament: "How Comes It that we all start out Originals and end up Copies?" Upon situating our work in the world of experience and narrative, and in accepting the idea that we must start with a story in order to attribute meaning to and to give expression to our experience, we would have to reverse Trilling's question - How Comes It that we all start out Copies and end up Originals? To this question, Geertz finds an answer that is "surprisingly reassuring: it is the copying that originates." (1986, p.380)

We have little choice but to start out with copies. We cannot perform meaning in our lives without situating our experience in stories. Stories are, in the first place, given. However, it is the relative indeterminacy - the ambiguity and uncertainty - of all stories that we can only negotiate through recourse to our lived experience and our imagination. And this requires that we engage in a process of "origination".

The following discussion presents some thoughts about the structure of a context of training/supervision that is framed by these ideas on narrative or story.

TRAINING AND SUPERVISION IN THE WORLD OF NARRATIVE AND EXPERIENCE

Training and supervision has raised a dilemma for those teachers/supervisors who have concerns that such contexts can be subjugating to participants - concerns that the training context might encourage participants to surrender their own "hard-won" knowledges and submit to the authority of the teacher/supervisor; concerns that participants could be incited to discipline themselves and shape their "life as therapist" according to certain specifications; concerns that participants might fashion their lives as recruits. Is there a solution to this dilemma? Is it possible to conceive of a process of training/supervision that doesn't have this outcome?

As previously argued, every supervision and training context is informed by specific ideas and their associated practices, and these ideas and practices will reflect the ideas and practices of a particular therapy of choice. If the candidate has had access to sufficient information about the frame for therapy and training/supervision, and proceeds with enrolment, it could be generally assumed that this fits, however loosely, with what s/he perceives to be preferred practices and values.[6]

Thus, I usually assume that, upon entering the training context, participants will expect me to encourage them to situate their work in a story about therapy that is informed by ideas about the world of experience and narrative. I also generally assume that participants will expect the context of supervision/training to be informed by this story.

However, such assumptions about the expectations of participants should not by any means allay all concerns about the possible subjugating nature of the processes of training/supervision. In what other ways can an orientation be established that mitigates against this possibility?

In regard to a story about therapy that is framed by the text analogy or narrative metaphor, it can be explicitly recognized that the readiness of the participant to at least temporarily situate his/her work in this story, and the encouragement of the participant, on behalf of the teacher/supervisor, to "copy" this story, provides only a point of entry from which a new journey can be undertaken; that the story about therapy is not the journey itself.

In time, the journey becomes a thing in itself, however much its initial shape was borrowed from the past. The virtual text becomes a story of its own ... not the actual text ... but the text that the reader has constructed under its sway. (J. Bruner 1986, p.36-37)

The recognition of this fact encourages teachers/supervisors and participants to attend to the extent to which they are engaging in a performance of meaning under the guidance of the story.

It is not the participant's attempt to copy and the teacher/supervisor's encouragement for her/him to do so that is problematic. Of necessity, for any such endeavour there is always a starting point - a point of entry - and this is always with a "copy". However, complications do arise if teachers/

supervisors and participants believe that it is possible for participants to succeed in their attempts to copy, and if they believe that this is being achieved. This belief will blind participants and teachers/supervisors to what the participants are originating in their own work, and how they are doing this.[7] Thus, paradoxically, participants are most likely to experience success when they are faced with unique outcomes in their work that are enabling to families, and acknowledge the failure of their attempts to copy - when they experience, first hand, the phenomenon that Geertz (1986) finds "surprisingly reassuring: it is the copying that originates".

It is in the management of the indeterminate nature of any story about therapy, in the performance of meaning under the guidance of the story, that participants take this story over and make it their own. They must recruit their own lived experience and imagination to fill the gaps in the story, and resolve, for themselves, any inconsistencies and contradictions. In this process, the story about therapy is re-authored, and the participant's "life as therapist" is transformed.

These considerations raise questions of a general nature to be considered by teachers/supervisors and participants alike. To what extent does any particular training/supervision context:
- allow for and invite the incorporation of and facilitate the expression of aspects of the participants' lived experience?
- recruit the participants' imagination?
- encourage participants to identify what they are originating in their attempts to copy?
- enable participants to grasp the ways that they are taking over the story about therapy and making it their own?
- assist participants to explore the real effects of the performance of this story in their life as therapist?

THE STRUCTURE OF TRAINING AND SUPERVISION

In following the proposal that good stories are those that are more readily entered into by the reader - those that are more effective in encouraging the incorporation of the reader's maps, and those that are more successful in recruiting the reader's lived experience and imagination

– literary theorists have explored the structure of good stories. In assuming that what holds true for a good novel also holds true for a good story about therapy, it becomes possible for us to consider the structure of a good story about training/supervision.

We could assume that a good story about training/supervision will be supported by a structure that is effective in encouraging participants to enter into the story and to take it over and to make it their own. Such a structure would facilitate the expression of vital aspects of the participants' lived experience, and would trigger their imagination. We could also assume that if the attention of participants is brought to bear on the extent to which this is occuring, they will become aware of the extent to which they are involved in the process of origination; in both "the production and the comprehension of this work's intention". (Iser 1978, p.21)

And we could further assume that if participants are invited to attend to the specific details of how they are originating, that they would be in a better position to know which steps to take next in the further development of their own work. Clarity as to what future step might be worthwhile is arrived at through a perception of the unfolding of unique developments through the recent history of one's own work.

Here I will present some thoughts about a structure for training/supervision that I believe to reflect these assumptions.

Unique Outcomes and Life as Therapist Retold

The teacher/supervisor can be alert to all unique developments or outcomes that are occuring in the participants' work. The observation of participants in "live interviews" and on videotapes of interviews provides the ideal opportunity for this. Unique outcomes are those that the teacher/supervisor believes clearly facilitate, for those persons who seek therapy, the re-authoring of lives according to preferred stories, and are developments that might not have been exactly or generally predicted by the teacher/supervisor. These unique outcomes constitute the more "sparkling events" of the interview.

Once identified, participants can be encouraged to attend to the significance of these unique outcomes, and, in the process, be engaged in a re-authoring of their own stories about therapy, and of their stories about their "life as therapist". To assist in this, teachers/supervisors can interview the participants after their interviews with families. At this time participants can be invited to speculate about what made the unique outcomes in their work possible. How did these unique outcomes relate to aspects of their lived experience, and/or what was it about the interview that triggered their imagination in this way? What made the unique outcomes possible? The teacher/supervisor can ask other questions about what the participants think this unique outcome might reflect about them as therapists, and about what it might say about their own particular interviewing "styles". Yet another category of questions can be introduced to encourage the participants to review what all of this might suggest about future directions in their work.[8] As the training/supervision proceeds, teachers/supervisors can encourage participants to respond to what they perceive to be unique outcomes in the work of others in the group.

Griemas and Courtes (1976) propose that all stories exist in a dual landscape - the landscape of action and the landscape of consciousness.[9] The first is the landscape upon which events unfold; the context into which events must be plotted in order to be rendered meaningful or significant. Those questions that bring forth the participants' lived experience and imagination as the context of the unique outcomes can be considered landscape of action questions.

The landscape of consciousness is the landscape that represents the inner world of the protagonists in the story, and includes what they felt, thought and perceived, and the realizations and conclusions arrived at in relation to the developments unfolding in the landscape of action. Those questions that encourage participants to speculate about what the unique outcomes in their work might reflect about them as therapists, and about what it might say about their own particular interviewing "styles", can be considered landscape of consciousness questions.

Unique Counselling Careers

Not only do persons come to family therapy training with specific and influential expectations about the supervision/training context, but they also come with a story about what I will call their "counselling career". This story can also have a highly significant effect on the course of supervision and training and, thus, is worthy of special consideration.

On those occasions when I have had the time and the opportunity to enquire about the histories of the counselling careers of participants of training courses, most have responded with a rather restricted mundane and general account of this. In these accounts, details about the more formal aspects of the counselling career usually predominate. These details include information about the college/university that the person attended, the courses taken, the diplomas/degrees conferred, and the history of their employment.

When asked about how this history might have contributed to the decision to enrol in family therapy training, by far the greater number of participants have referred to shortcomings: they were confronted with the realization that they were ill-equipped to do the job they were hired to do, or were disappointed with what they had to offer the families that sought their help.

Dissatisfied with the general and formal nature of these accounts, I decided to ask participants questions that I believed could bring forth a more unique account of their counselling careers. Some of these questions were about the nature of personal crises that participants had experienced in these careers; about what triggered these crises, about how redress was achieved, about the new realizations and conclusions that became available during and subsequent to redress, and about the real effects of these realizations and conclusions on the shape of the participants' counselling careers. In response to these questions, participants became active in the attribution of new meaning to their counselling careers and, in contrast to the formal accounts, generated alternative accounts that accommodated the various turning points in the histories of these careers.

Considering other ways that the stories of their counselling careers might be told clearly provided, for participants, new understandings and new possibilities.

... any story one may tell about anything is better understood by considering other possible ways in which it can be told. That must surely be as true of the life stories we tell as of any others. In that case, we have come full round to the ancient homily that the only life worth living is the well-examined one. But it puts a different meaning on the homily. If we can learn how people put their narratives together when they tell stories from life, considering as well how they might have proceeded, we might then have contributed something new to that great ideal. (J. Bruner 1987, p.32)

I was also dissatisfied with the "enrolment stories" that were offered by most of these participants - they seemed so devoid of what could be considered the more "sparkling" facts. Did the histories of their counselling careers really set them so far apart from the story about therapy that informed the course they had enrolled in? Surely not. Most participants had some knowledge of the ideas and of the structure of the training context into which they were entering. I decided to ask other questions about how the participants' own discoveries in the histories of their counselling careers might connect them to the story that was privileged in the training context; about the possible links between their unique realizations and conclusions and the story that informed the course into which they had decided to enrol. In response to these questions, participants seemed able to more freely incorporate important aspects of their counselling experience into the story about therapy that was privileged in the training context.

At a later date, those participants whom I'd had the opportunity to interview in this way informed me that this retelling of their story about their counselling careers had real effects that were positive. These real effects concerned not just their work, but also their lives and relationships more generally. This should not be so surprising. In some ways, these accounts of counselling careers can be thought of as encapsulated autobiographies, and it could be expected that the re-authoring of these would have such general effects.

In further discussion with participants about their experience of these retellings, the extent to which the performance of alternative stories is shaping of lives and relationships became more evident to them. This is a form of personal research that J. Bruner (1987) strongly argues for:

I cannot imagine a more important psychological research project than one that addresses itself to the 'development of autobiography' - how our way of telling about ourselves changes, and how these accounts come to take control of our ways of life. Yet, I know of not a single comprehensive study on this subject. (p.15)

Although participants were enthusiastic about this exercise, restrictions on my time discouraged me from widening its scope. Then, in a telephone conversation, Karl Tomm mentioned that he had instituted a project in which he was encouraging participants in the University of Calgary Family Therapy Program to interview each other about their counselling histories, and that the feedback he had received about this was highly reinforcing on this project. I decided to follow suit, suggesting to participants that they interview each other with a focus on unique counselling careers.

Details of Exercise

My practice is to suggest that this exercise be undertaken in groups of three to five persons, and fashioned after the reflecting team structure. One group member volunteers to be interviewed about their counselling career, another volunteers to do the interviewing, and the others participate as members of the reflecting team. The exercise should be unhurried and, over the course of training, each group member should have the opportunity to rotate through the various roles.

Experience suggests that this exercise should not be attempted until participants are familiar with the ideas that provide a frame for it, and not before they believe that they are ready to experiment with situating their work in the context of these ideas. Any forseeable complications to the exercise should be addressed beforehand. For example, it is advisable to place into a separate group any participant who is hierarchically superior to another participant from the same place of work.

In this exercise, the interviewers and the members of the reflecting team are invited to address themselves to two primary tasks. The first has to do with the identification of the more sparkling facts of the interviewee's counselling career. This can be achieved through a review of the various crises and turning points in the interviewee's counselling history, of the unique realizations and conclusions that were triggered at these times, and of the subsequent effect of these on the direction of their counselling careers.

The second task for the interviewer and the reflecting team members is to encourage the interviewee to help them understand how the more sparkling facts of his/her counselling history connect to the ideas and practices that they found in the training course into which they had enrolled; to encourage the interviewee to contribute to their understanding of how the trajectory of her/his counselling career might have led to a point of intersection with the training course.

The Structure of Good Stories

One measure of a therapy that is consistent with the ideas presented in this paper would be the extent to which it provides, for those who seek it, an opportunity for the re-authoring of lives and relationships. Elsewhere, in drawing an analogy between a therapy of this form and good stories, I have proposed a "therapy of literary merit" (White 1988). In the exploring of this analogy I have considered various contributions made by literary theorists to the study of the structure of good stories.

I have also encouraged the participants of supervision/training to undertake their own study of good stories. I usually suggest that they first meet together in small groups of three to four members and select a relatively well-known novel that they believe they might enjoy reading. After each member has read this novel, I suggest that they reconvene and apply themselves to the following tasks:

- To identify and discuss their experiences of reading the novel, concentrating on the various levels at which they felt engaged in or absorbed by the story, and on how they identified with certain characters in the story.
- To determine the significant differences between members, in terms of their experiences and understandings of the text; in terms of their different readings or versions of the story. This contributes to an awareness of the extent to which they are active in the derivation of unique interpretations of their worlds, and in the construction of these worlds.
- To review the highly specific ways that members entered into the story, took it over, and made it their own. This would include discussion of what aspects of their lived experience made this possible, and of how their imagination featured in the production of their unique accounts.
- To consider how the author structured the story, and which elements of this structure seemed most successful in inviting the members into the story; which elements seemed most effective or compelling in recruiting their imagination and lived experience.

Following this exercise, the teacher/supervisor can review the contributions of various literary theorists to an understanding of the structure of texts of literary merit[10], and participants can be encouraged to compare their own findings with these.

Participants can then be engaged in discussions about how this research might be relevant to the structuring of a context for therapy which would provide, for those who seek it, the opportunity to re-author their lives and their relationships; an opportunity to enter into alternative stories about their lives and relationships, to take these stories over, and to make them their own. This would be a context in which the therapist participates as co-author, but also one in which people are encouraged to assume the role of the privileged author of their own lives.

CONCLUSION

In these notes, I have discussed ideas that relate to the world of experience and narrative. These ideas set the frame for a particular orientation to therapy and to training and supervision. I have presented some thoughts about how this frame can contribute to an approach to the structure of supervision and training.

Apart from the specific ideas and practices that inform the structure of training/supervision, there are other factors to be considered by therapists before proceeding with enrolment into a course or prior to contracting supervision. One such factor is the extent to which the therapist will be able to arrange the necessary space in their own workplace to perform the therapy that is preferred in the training/supervision context of choice.

A decision to enter a training/supervision context is one that will often require the therapist to separate from - at least temporarily - other ideas and practices that have been informing their work. It is unhelpful for therapists to consider this a requirement to discard, betray or disqualify their lived experience of therapy. Instead, it can be seen as an invitation to therapists to entertain a different "frame" for this lived experience - not just one that brings with it lenses for new ways of "seeing" the world and new possibilities in therapy, but also one that can only be authenticated for the therapist through the expression of their own lived experience.

Although therapists may be enthusiastic about the extent to which the frame that is privileged in a particular training/supervision context provides a unique - perhaps even radical - shift in the ordering of their therapy, it is important that they maintain some awareness of the fact that, as with those other frames that have gone before, the world is actually constructed through this "new" frame. This awareness assists persons to review the real effects and limitations, and perhaps even the dangers, of the frame that is privileged in the chosen training/supervision context.

Throughout the discussion of the structure of training and supervision, I chose to focus primarily on the implications, for participants, of a particular structure of training and supervision. However, as the collaborative aspects of this work become more evident, the distinction teacher/supervisor/participant breaks down. Thus, in this paper, I could have equally focussed on the experience of the teacher/supervisor as, needless to say, such a frame and structure has real effects on their "life as teacher/supervisor", as they perform and re-perform their story about therapy and training/supervision; as they experience and re-experience that "it is the copying that originates".

NOTES

1. Victor Turner (1982) wrote that these expressions are "... the crystallized secretions of once living experience". (p.17)

2. By arguing for the proposal about the extent to which stories determine the meaning attributed to experience, I am not suggesting that the context of our lives is single-storied. Rather, I believe the context of our lives is multi-storied. There is a range of alternative stories for the interpretation of experience in which we and others may situate our lives. Also, despite this assertion about the story-determined nature of meaning, it turns out (as discussed later) that all such stories are in fact indeterminate.

3. When discussing the performative aspects of the ritual process, Turner (1980) states: "The term 'performance' is, of course, derived from Old English parfournu, literally, 'to furnish completely or thoroughly'. To perform is thus to bring something about, to consumate something, or to 'carry out' a play, order, or project. But in the carrying out, I hold, something new may be generated. The performance transforms itself." (p.160)

4. Turner (1980), when discussing the ritual process, relates indeterminacy to the subjunctive mood of verb:
"Indeterminacy is, so to speak, in the subjunctive mood, since it is that which is not yet settled, concluded, and known. It is all that may be, might be, could be, perhaps even should be ... Sally Falk Moore goes so far as to suggest that 'the underlying quality of social life should be considered to be one of theoretical absolute indeterminacy'."
This relation of indeterminacy to the subjunctive mood is also discussed by J. Bruner (1986).

5. For further discussion of those aspects of the structure of stories that encourage the reader to enter the story, to take it over and make to it their own, see J. Bruner (1986).

6. However, this is not always the case. Sometimes a person's decision to enter a particular training/supervision context is based primarily on other reasons - for example, those that are political in nature (prestige, requirements of employer, advancement of career, etc.) and/or the fact that there is a limited range of alternatives available for training/supervision. This argues for the importance of the availability of a range of training/supervision contexts.

7. This belief will also blind teachers and supervisors to the evolving nature of their own work as they "tell it and retell it".

8. For examples of such questions, see "The process of questioning: A therapy of literary merit?" (White 1988).

9. Elsewhere, in proposing a therapy of literary merit, and in referring to therapy as a process of questioning, I have referred to Griemas' and Courtes' proposal (White 1988).

10. Jerome Bruner (1986) provides an excellent review of these contributions in his book "Actual Minds, Possible Worlds".

REFERENCES

Bruner, E. 1986:
   Experience and its expressions. In Turner, V. & Bruner, E. (Eds.): **The Anthropology of Experience**. Chicago; University of Illinois Press.
Bruner, J. 1986:
   Actual Minds, Possible Worlds. Massachusetts; Harvard University Press.
Bruner, J. 1987:
   Life as narrative. **Social Research**, 54(1).
Dilthey, W. 1976:
   Dilthey: Selected writings (Ed. H. Rickman). Cambridge; Cambridge University Press.
Geertz, C. 1983:
   Local Knowledge: Further essays in Interpretive anthropology. New York; Basic Books.
Geertz, C. 1986:
   Making experiences, authoring selves. In Turner, V. & Bruner, E. (Eds.): **The Anthropology of Experience**. Chicago; University of Illinois Press.
Griemas, A. & Courtes, J. 1976:
   The cognitive dimension of narrative discourse. **New Literary History**, 7:433-447.

Iser, W. 1978:
The Act of Reading. Baltimore; John Hopkins, University Press.
Ricoeur, P. 1983:
Time and Narrative. Chicago; University of Chicago Press.
Turner, V. 1980:
Social dramas and stories about them.**Critical Inquiry**, Autumn, pp.141-168.
Turner, V. 1982:
From Ritual to Theatre. New York; Performing Arts Press.
White, M. 1988:
The process of questioning: A therapy of literary merit?**Dulwich Centre Newsletter**, Winter, pp.8-14.
White, M. 1988/89:
The externalizing of the problem and the re-authoring of lives and relationships. **Dulwich Centre Newsletter**, Summer, pp.3-21.
White, M. 1989:
Introduction. In Epston, D. & White, M., **Literate Means to Therapeutic Ends**. Adelaide; Dulwich Centre Publications.

CHAPTER V

A PROBLEM OF BELONGING

Jeremy* & David Epston

Previously published in the "Story Corner" section of Australian & New Zealand Journal of Family Therapy 1989, Vol.10, No.2.

(*Jeremy prefers to maintain his anonymity)

Jeremy, aged 16, his father, Roy, and his step-mother, Raewyn, entered my room silently. They seated themselves in front of me: Jeremy looked utterly downcast; Roy had steeled himself for something or other; and Raewyn - seven months pregnant - had an air about her of the keenest sadness. I was surprised when Jeremy answered my question: "What's brought you folks to a person like me?" He said, "It's my fault ... it's the way I've been treating them ... I've been unfair ... I've betrayed their trust ... I lied to them about smashing Roy's watch and Raewyn's tennis racket ... I've been nasty to Raewyn." When his confession was completed, Roy, avoiding eye-contact with either Raewyn or Jeremy, said that he had made his mind up. It had been a difficult decision for him, but some books he had read had helped him come to his conclusion. As it had come to a choice for him between his son and his wife, he had decided in favour of Raewyn. Roy's declaration seemed to deepen Raewyn's despair and she looked downwards.

I asked if I could learn the story of this problem. Roy took over for a while. He and Jeremy's mother had separated in 1979. Roy and Raewyn married in 1985. Jeremy had been living with his mother, but had joined his father and Raewyn in September of 1987. Once again, Jeremy took up the story. "I didn't get on with Mum ... she shut me out ... I was like a boarder ... she was always crying wolf to Dad." When I asked, "Were you an orphan in your own home?" everyone nodded in agreement. Jeremy had spent his school holidays with his father and Raewyn. When I asked about his reunion with his father, Jeremy said: "They included me ... they listened to me ... they didn't push me away." Raewyn met my eyes and began to speak: "He was very lonely ... very hurt ... he wasn't able to express himself or his feelings. It was almost as if he was starved ... he would follow me around. We spent a lot of time together." I asked Raewyn and Jeremy if he had filled himself up with love and affection. They both agreed that he had over a period of three months, and at that time their relationship suited them both. However, around February/March of 1988, Raewyn observed that Jeremy had become moody and started to withdraw. By August, Raewyn found Jeremy offensive, arrogant, "putting me down", and came finally to fear for her well-being. She said that he had become "a monster". Still they had been able to weather these storms until Raewyn's broken tennis racket and Roy's smashed wrist-watch were found hidden underneath Jeremy's bed. They had interrogated him about this, but all he did was "lie".

Experience, Contradiction, Narrative & Imagination

This was the last straw, the straw that had broken Roy's determination to make a home for his son and, perhaps, to make up for Jeremy's neglect by his mother. But both Jeremy and Raewyn just looked dismayed.

I asked when Roy and Raewyn had decided on their pregnancy. The mood lifted a bit as they related the events surrounding it. Roy had had a vasectomy reversed and "there was a lot of talk about that". When that was successful, it was some months before a pregnancy ensued. This was followed by a search for a special name until they found one to suit them, "a long-sought-after one".

It then dawned on everyone that around about the time of the vasectomy discussion, Jeremy had commenced his withdrawal. Everyone was both aghast and relieved. "Did you feel you were losing your belonging, a belonging that was newfound?" I asked. Jeremy agreed. "Would you have guessed, Roy and Raewyn, that the vasectomy and pregnancy could have led Jeremy to doubt his belonging?" They hadn't thought of that, but they were now. I asked Jeremy if his violence towards the property of Roy and Raewyn might be an expression of his anger at thinking he would lose his place, the place where, at long last, he had come home to himself. He said that he thought that was quite possible.

In summary, I asked each and every one of them to consider their futures carefully: "Roy and Raewyn, can you officially 'belong' Jeremy or is it too late? ... has there been too much water under the bridge? ... Jeremy, are you prepared to be a candidate for their 'belonging' or is it too late? ... has there been too much water under the bridge?" I requested that this matter be reflected on by both parties before any decisions were reached, and invited them to return in a month's time to inform me of the outcome.

I was very eager to see them again, but just meeting them at the door gave it away. They looked so 'belonged' that I didn't even need to enquire as to what decision they had all reached. Jeremy reported that he "felt a lot more relaxed ... a lot more part of the family ... and not so much of a stranger". Raewyn with great pleasure announced that the problem was "totally gone". Roy joked that "it felt like I was the meat in the sandwich ... I was being bitten from both sides". Jeremy had immediately recommenced eating and sleeping after our first session and, as he put it, was "giving friends more time". He said that "there was anger and fear that I would never be part of the family again ... it was like running around and going

A Problem of Belonging

nowhere ... I just got more lost in it ... now I have found a way out of it ... if I hadn't escaped, I would have closed in on myself and become a stranger to everyone".

We all agreed that it might be helpful to Jeremy and to others for him to write his story. The rest of the session was spent coming up with ideas for his story. Everyone contributed.

The following letter summarizes this discussion:

Dear Jeremy,

Here is a summary of the proposal for your story:
1. *When did you start fearing that you were losing your belonging to your newfound family? Roy and Raewyn discussing a reversal of his vasectomy? Getting the vasectomy reversed? Raewyn announcing her pregnancy?*
2. *What did this fear lead to? Confusion; anger; fear of expressing your true feelings to your Dad and Raewyn; loss of appetite; disinterest in your friends; not sleeping; grumpiness.*
3. *This culminated in acts of symbolic violence (e.g. watch, tennis racket), and led Raewyn to fear for her well-being as she believed you had turned into a "monster", and led Roy to "feel I had to mediate between two warring factions" and feel he was being tested as to his loyalty: his loyalty to his son or loyalty to his wife. At the same time, Jeremy, you were "trying to hang on to what little I had left (my Dad)".*
4. *Visit to the Family Therapy Centre.*
5. *What happened for you, Jeremy: "I found a way out ... it cleared the confusion!" How did this happen?*
   - "It started to make sense to me and Roy and Raewyn."
   - "I had felt I was going crazy."

Now "I am dealing with anger better"; no longer so agitated by your mother's carelessness; "relationships between me and Raewyn and me and Roy have been repaired"; "have started stating my own opinions with Dad, and am even listening better"; developed maturity in many ways; and attracted the attention once again of your many friends.

Jeremy, this is merely an outline of events as we all talked your story over. Feel free to add, subtract, amend as much as you wish. It's your story, but I just thought the above might be helpful to provide you with a story line.

Many thanks too, Jeremy, on behalf of other young people and their families who will be assisted in hearing about your experiences and how you all turned what might have been a tragic story into a success story. Fond regards, D.E.

Experience, Contradiction, Narrative & Imagination

A month later, I received a card from Raewyn announcing the birth of their long sought after son. She wryly commented that the only problem was a competition between them all to mother the baby.

Another month later, Jeremy's story arrived and I read it with great interest:

This is my account of some problems I had in fitting in with a new family. When I was about seven, my parents were divorced. For a couple of years, my father Roy, my sister, and I lived together. After that, my sister and I moved in with my mother, Donna. My life with my mother was quite unsettled. We were always moving from house to house, always because of her money problems and more importantly, I had a bad relationship with her. She is a very selfish and uncaring person, who never cares about anybody else but expects everyone to care for her. She rejected and neglected me a lot. She would never show any real affection for me. She used my sister to gang up on me and was constantly putting me down. When we got into arguments, she would blame my father for our standard of living and my "uncontrollable behaviour". She made Roy out to be the architect of all her troubles.

Finally, when I was fifteen, the whole thing literally blew up. One day in the August holidays, I had an accident with a can of petrol while filling up the lawn-mower, and the garage at my mother's place caught fire. When she came home, her first concern was not for me but for the garage. In other words, she was thinking of herself. It was at that moment that I realised just how selfish and uncaring she really was. I just wanted to get away; I wanted to be dead. She then rang up Roy and blamed him for what I had done. She was just pathetic. Finally I was taken away from it all. Roy took me home with him and asked me to live with him and Raewyn, his wife. Finally I was in an environment where I was cared about, and I felt like I belonged. During these first few months, I spent a lot of time with Raewyn and became very close to her.

Then about six months later, Roy and Raewyn decided to have a baby. Secretly, this threatened me and threw my belonging in this new family into question. Around this time my mood started to change. I became aggressive and withdrawn. I didn't really notice this change myself. The person who saw it happening the most was Raewyn. Because she had chosen to accept me into her life, I looked upon her as a sort of mother substitute, and unfortunately, because of this, a lot of my aggression was directed at her. I undertook acts of symbolic violence, such as breaking and stealing things, and then hiding them in my room. I was always crabby and moody. I started to lose my appetite. My relationships with other people deteriorated. Finally it came to a head.

Roy and Raewyn found the things I had broken and stolen from around the house. They asked me why I had done this and why I was so aggressive and nasty. I couldn't answer this. It's not that I didn't want to, but I just couldn't find the answer. After much discussion, we decided to start over again and try to forget what had happened. But this didn't work, and my aggressive behaviour kept up. Raewyn began to even fear for her safety. She thought I had turned into a monster. Roy and Raewyn began to give up on me and decided to - in a way - reject me from their family.

This hurt me a lot. I never went out with them any more and we wouldn't talk together. I spent more and more time on my own and started to turn into a hermit. I saw my friends less; I slept and ate less and had no interest in anything. I was incredibly confused. It was like I was running around a lot, looking for a way out, but getting nowhere. I became more and more depressed.

After a while of this, Roy and Raewyn decided that the situation needed outside help. I didn't really worry about this - I was almost past caring. All three of us went to The Family Therapy Centre. It was here that my problem was finally made clear to me. I had been rejected so much by my mother, and I never wanted that to happen to me again. Roy and Raewyn had given me a place where I felt belonged. I thought that them having a baby would mean that my place would be taken and I would no longer belong with them. It made me angry. I didn't want to be treated like my mother treated me, like a boarder in my own home. This was my problem. I saw it, and Roy and Raewyn saw it, and we all understood it. This was a tremendous weight off my mind. I saw my way out and I belonged once more back in the family.

On the 5th of March, 1989, Raewyn gave birth to a baby boy. This sort of signalled the end of our crisis. The baby no longer threatens me. He is part of the family. I can now talk to Roy and Raewyn; I have started to listen more and even voice my own opinion now and again. I sleep and eat better and have become more available to my friends. In its own way, this crisis has brought the family closer together than ever.

Yours sincerely, Jeremy.

P.S.: Please excuse the lateness of my story.

I replied immediately:

Experience, Contradiction, Narrative & Imagination

Dear Jeremy,

There is no need to apologize for the lateness of your story. It was well worth waiting for. And perhaps you had to wait for Fergus' arrival to see if things would work out for you as you had hoped. Raewyn wrote me not so long ago telling me about Fergus and that you and your Dad are doing a lot of mothering of him.

Jeremy, I was deeply touched by your story because it is an inspiring one. With your permission, I will revise it only by changing everyone's names and find ways to make it available to other professional helpers or people and families who are grappling with their belonging like you, Roy, and Raewyn did. For my part, I am very pleased to have been a witness to your belonging them and their belonging of you. In all my contact with you, I was struck by your sensitivity to others and yourself and your 'old head' on relatively young shoulders. If I were to predict your future, I would predict a very good one for you, especially in the realm of relationships and friendships. My guess is that as your belonging story becomes the dominant one in your life, your boarder story will become more and more submerged and overlooked. I believe that as time goes by, you will be a very good and sensitive friend, colleague, and lover to your friends, colleagues, and lovers.

Best wishes for a future determined by your new belonging story. It was a privilege to have known you, Roy, and Raewyn.

Yours with best wishes, D.E.

CHAPTER VI

SELF-SPECIALIZATION

Bryce Wilson* & David Epston

*Previously published in the "Story Corner" section of
Australian & New Zealand Journal of Family Therapy
1989, Vol.10, No.2.*

(* Bryce can be contacted c/- David Epston.)

Mrs Wilson rang very concerned about the future of her family. Her relationship with her only child, Bryce, had deteriorated to the point where silence now prevailed between them. Mr Wilson had taken over the talking with Bryce, but now he too was considering adopting silence. In fact, Mrs Wilson considered that the matter was so urgent that she insisted we meet immediately even though Mr Wilson was unable to attend. I agreed to her request, but insisted that the session be video-taped so that Mr Wilson could catch up with events on his home-coming.

Bryce was an extraordinary 14 year old and it was immediately obvious to me that I should speak to him as my equal. Bryce very clearly knew his own mind and found himself very impatient with those he presumed didn't. He had few, if any, friends at school which he put down to his overwhelming desire to correct them. He was finding himself increasingly in trouble at school with the teaching staff. He had straight A's in Ability and straight D's in Performance. And he was only too willing to admit that his relationships with his parents had reached an all time low.

The following is a summary of our meeting:

Dear Bryce,

I was interested to meet you today and as agreed am writing a summary of our discussions.

It sounds as if you have become a self-specialist, enjoying your own company and preferring your own mind. In a manner of speaking you have become your own fan club. No wonder you experience an urgency to correct others, to put them right when they appear wrong to you. Although I can easily imagine many of your age-mates would be drawn to your ability, you obviously have found ways to repel them. You tell me that more recently you "are learning not to correct others or put them down" by "slowing down my thinking process before talking". By giving yourself some time to reflect on the consequences, you have restrained yourself from correcting others. You haven't yet had the urge to promote others' abilities or coach them even though you know that others "would think I was an improved person". There is a hazard in self-specialization you probably hadn't considered before going to boarding school. You may have specialised in your thinking at the expense of your emotional development. As I said, I have found many scholars to be emotional juveniles. It's almost as if in self-specialising, they have become self-sensitive and insensitive to others and their feelings. Bryce, you softened ever since your boarding school experience when you discovered your

Experience, Contradiction, Narrative & Imagination

sensitivity to others (your mum and your dad). The other hazard worth considering is making a fool of yourself at school by being A in ability and D in performance. This enrages teachers, as you well know, and sooner or later they may be tempted to take revenge on you. Although you may think you are making a fool of them, in fact, you may be making a fool of yourself.

You tell me that you and your father have entered into an "I'm all right / you're all wrong" relationship.[1] Your father took over from your mother when, I imagine, it looked as if you were all right (and she was all wrong) in regard to her as a person. If this continues, your son-father relationship as well as your son-mother relationship could deteriorate over time until no-one can be bothered talking to you. If you can convince either of them they are all wrong, then they have nothing to say to you. The casualties from such a purported victory may be more than you have anticipated.

Ben Cole[2] had some similar experiences, and he and I wrote a story about it. I am including it in the hope that it may be useful to you in considering what you want to make of yourself in life: a self-specialist or a person who specialises in others as well as in themself. It is worth considering carefully now what kind of future you want to design for yourself.

I look forward to discussing this further with you when you are ready.

Best wishes, D.E.

We all met together several weeks later. Bryce said he "had seen the light" and had already made amends with both his parents, much to their relief and delight. Everyone agreed that the problems that had brought them to this agency had dissolved. We reviewed this in some detail. Bryce agreed to summarise his thoughts in writing. Four months later, I received the following:

I was perfect. I was bright and good at sports and the most special thing about me was I was never wrong. Then why was I always fighting with parents and friends? It can't have been my fault; I'm never wrong. It seemed that everyone else in the world was useless.

This problem I had was something called self-specialization. I found myself so interesting and perfect. I was the only person I took an interest in!

How do you 'fix' the problem? Firstly you must take a good long look at yourself and want to change. It's not difficult. Try listening to other people for a change. Support their ideas and give them encouragement. You will feel a much better person for it. Try to avoid your own thoughts and just listen. Make a few mistakes on purpose and then apologise. Learning to apologise and admit that you are wrong is the first major step to opening up and becoming a new and better, caring person.

Do you find yourself interesting? Do you think that you are always right? Maybe on a smaller scale.

Believe me, self-specialization is not a good habit. You can 'fix' something that may only be minor at the moment but it has the potential to become very major. For example, you could end up with no communication with your parents. Simply because you think you are always right. I've been down that road and am now changing. I just hope you take heed of this advice and give it a try!

Just listen to an expert to get help. Not yourself!

Bryce reviewed the above a year later and provided this summary:

Sorry, I haven't been able to return your original sooner, but Fifth Form doesn't leave much time for other things.

Every now and then, I have a fight with my parents. But most teenagers tend to clash with them every now and then.

Recently I have been able to mix with a wider scope of people. I am still finding my ground. But, until then, I seem to be able to fit into any social group without upsetting anybody. That is a complete reversal to when I came to you. I can mix with people, but still have time to do a few activities by myself.

Thanks for your help and advice. Good luck to anyone else like myself in the future. *Regards, B.W.*

NOTES

1. I am indebted to Michael White for this relationship description.

2. Epston, D. & Cole, B. 1986/7: Are you a candidate for mental karate training? **Dulwich Centre Newsletter**, Summer, pp.6-7.

CHAPTER VII

DECONSTRUCTION AND THERAPY

Michael White

*Previously published in
Dulwich Centre Newsletter
1991, No.3.*

Parts of this paper were presented at the End of Grand Designs conference in Heidelberg, April 1991, and at the Generating Possibilities Through Therapeutic Conversations Conference in Tulsa, Oklahoma in June 1991.

Lest some readers be disappointed, before proceeding with my discussion of deconstruction and therapy I should inform you that this paper is not about the deconstruction of the knowledges and the practices of specific and established models of therapy, or about the deconstruction of any particular therapy "movement". Rather, in this paper I have chosen to cast certain practices of therapy within the frame provided by deconstruction.

As the first and foremost concern of my professional life relates to what happens in the therapeutic context, at the outset of this paper I will present several stories of therapy. I would like to emphasize the fact that, due to space considerations, these stories are glossed. They do not adequately represent the disorderly process of therapy - the ups and downs of that adventure that we refer to as therapy. Thus, there is a simplicity reflected in these accounts that cannot be found in the work itself.

Elizabeth

Elizabeth, a sole parent[1], initially consulted me about her two daughters, aged twelve and fifteen years. She was concerned about their persistent antagonism towards her, their frequent tantrums, their abuse of her, and their apparent unhappiness. These problems had been upsetting to Elizabeth for some considerable time, and she was concerned that she might never recover from the despair that she was experiencing. She had come to the interview alone because her children refused to accompany her. As Elizabeth described these problems to me, she revealed that she had begun to experience what she thought might be "hate" for them, and this had been distressing her all the more.

When discussing with Elizabeth her concerns, I first asked about how these problems were affecting the lives of family members, and about the extent to which they were interfering in family relationships. I then asked more specifically about how these problems had been influencing her thoughts about herself: What did she believe these problems reflected about her as a parent? What conclusions had she come to about herself as a mother? Tearfully, Elizabeth confessed that she had concluded that she was a failure as a mother. With this disclosure, I began to understand something of the private story that Elizabeth had been living by.

I then inquired as to how the view that she was a failure was compelling of Elizabeth in her relationship with her children. In response to this question, she gave details of the guilt that she experienced over not having sustained a "more ideal" family environment, of her highly tenuous and apologetic interaction with her daughters, and of the extent to which she felt bound to submit herself to their evaluation of her.

Was the havoc that the view of failure, and its associated guilt, was wreaking in her life and her relationships acceptable to her? Or would Elizabeth feel more comfortable if she broke her life and her relationships free of the tyranny of this view and its associated guilt? In response to these questions, Elizabeth made it clear, in no uncertain terms, that the current status of her relationship with her children was quite untenable, and that it was time for her to intervene and have more to say about the direction of her life and the shape of this relationship.

I encouraged Elizabeth to explore how she had been recruited into this view that she was a failure as a mother and as a person, and about the mechanisms by which her guilt had been provoked. What experiences had been most instrumental in this recruitment? Did she think that women were more vulnerable to being recruited into the view that they had failed their children, or was it more likely that men would be recruited into this view? On this point she had no doubt - women!

The exploration of these questions brought forth some of the specifics of Elizabeth's recruitment into the view that she was a failure (for example, her experience as the recipient of abuse at the hands of her former husband)[2], and the wider context of the gender-specific nature of this construction (for example, the inequitable social structures that reinforce this view for sole parents who are women, and the prevalence of mother-blaming in our culture).

As we explored the various ways that the view that she was a failure had affected her life, and some of the details of how she was recruited into this view, Elizabeth began to experience in herself an identity distinct in relation to this view - failure no longer spoke to her of her identity. This development cleared the way for us to distinguish some of the areas of her life that had not been co-opted by this view.

I partly facilitated the identification of these distinctions by providing Elizabeth with an account of the myriad of ways that the idea of failure, and its associated guilt, had tyrannized the lives of other women with whom I had talked - other women who had been subject to similar processes of recruitment. I then said that it was my understanding that this sort of tyrannization was never totally effective; that it had never entirely succeeded in eclipsing the lives of these women. I gave examples: "Some of these women had escaped the effects of this view of failure in their relationships with women friends, and others had kept alive their hopes that things could be different". In response to this, Elizabeth identified instances in several areas of her life in which she had been able to resist this tyranny.

I asked Elizabeth whether she thought this resistance was a positive or negative development in her life. As she said that this was a positive development, I inquired as to why she believed this to be so. During our subsequent discussion, it was determined that these instances reflected that she had not totally submitted to these negative views of who she was, and that she had some resolve to challenge the tyranny of guilt. This provided Elizabeth with evidence that her life had not been dominated by failure.

Then, through a series of questions, I encouraged Elizabeth to trace the history of this refusal. In the process of this, she identified a couple of historical figures who had witnessed some developments in her capacity to protest certain injustices. In our subsequent discussion, Elizabeth put both of us in touch with alternative versions of who she might be, versions of herself that she clearly preferred. As these alternative and preferred versions emerged from the shadows through our discussion, they became more available to Elizabeth to enter her life into.

As Elizabeth's enthusiasm for this alternative knowledge of who she was as a person became more apparent, I discussed with her the importance of seizing the initiative in putting others in touch with what she had discovered. To this end, I encouraged her to identify persons who might provide an appropriate audience to this other version of who she might be, persons who might participate in the acknowledgement of and the authentication of this version[3]. We then discussed various ideas about how she might introduce this other version of herself to these persons, and ideas about how these persons could be invited to respond to what Elizabeth was enthusiastic about in regard to these discoveries.

As part of the exploration of other versions of who Elizabeth might be, I had asked her to identify what it was about herself that she would personally like to have in a mother. Having articulated some details of this, I suggested that it might be important to catch her children up with this. Would she be prepared to tell them what she had discovered about herself as a woman and as a mother that she could appreciate, and to continue to remind them of this from time to time? This struck a chord. Elizabeth seemed rather joyful about the idea. I was quick to share my prediction that it was unlikely that Elizabeth's efforts to "reclaim her life" would be greeted at first with great enthusiasm by her children.

Elizabeth went away determined to have more to say about who she was, and to decline her children's invitations for her to subject herself to their constant evaluation and surveillance. Initially her daughters' response to her taking over the authorship of her own life was dramatic. They came up with some very creative ideas for turning back the clock. However, Elizabeth persevered through this, and then everyone's life went forward. She forged a new connection with her daughters, they became more enthusiastic about life, the abuse subsided, and Elizabeth reported that, for the first time, they had the sort of mother-daughter relationships that she had desired. They had become more connected as confidantes, able to discuss important matters of concern with each other.

Amy

Amy, aged 23 years, sought help in her struggle with anorexia nervosa. This was a longstanding problem, and it had withstood many attempts to resolve it. I first reviewed with Amy the effects that anorexia nervosa was having in the various domains of her life - including the social, the emotional, the intellectual, and, of course, the physical. In response to this review, the extent to which anorexia nervosa was making it difficult for her to make an appearance in any of these domains became apparent to both of us.

We then spent time exploring, in greater detail, how anorexia nervosa was affecting Amy's interactions with others. I wasn't surprised to learn that it had her constantly comparing herself to others, and that it had instilled in her a sense that she was being perpetually evaluated by others. Apart from this, it was enforcing a shroud of secrecy around her life, and isolating her from others.

How was the anorexia nervosa affecting Amy's attitude towards, and interaction with, herself? What was it requiring her to do to herself? Predictably, it was requiring her to watch over herself, to police herself. It had her engaging in operations on her own body, attempting to forge it into a shape that might be considered acceptable - a "docile body". And it had her punishing her own body for its transgressions.

I then engaged Amy in an investigation of how she had been recruited into these various practices, procedures and attitudes; these "disciplines of the self" according to gendered specifications for personhood; this hierarchical and disciplinary attitude and relationship to her own body. In this investigation, Amy was able to identify a history to this recruitment though familial, cultural and social contexts. In our subsequent discussion, anorexia nervosa appeared as the embodiment of these attitudes, practices and contexts.

Through this therapeutic process, anorexia nervosa was "unmasked", and Amy became increasingly alienated from it. The various taken-for-granted practices and attitudes that anorexia nervosa "relied upon for its survival" no longer spoke to her of the truth of who she was as a person. Would Amy be content to continue to submit to anorexia nervosa's claims on her life, to continue to defer to its requirements? Or was she more attracted to the idea of challenging its claims to her life, and to the idea of taking her life over and making it her own?

Amy had no hesitation in stating that it was time to make her life her own, so together we reviewed the available evidence that she might be able to do so: events that reflected resistance to the practices and attitudes upon which that state of "the government of self" called anorexia nervosa depended. This led to the identification of various developments or events that were of an anti-anorectic nature[4].

I asked Amy to evaluate these anti-anorectic developments: did she consider these to be the more attractive and desirable developments in her life, or did she consider them trivial and unappealing? In response, Amy judged these developments to be the preferred developments in her life. I then engaged her in a conversation about why she thought these developments were desirable, and about why she thought they personally suited her.

As Amy seemed to be more strongly supporting these anti-anorectic activities, I encouraged her to help me understand the basis or the foundation of these in her life. I also encouraged her to reflect upon what these preferred developments said about what she believed was important for her life. During the ensuing discussion, Amy began to more fully articulate a preferred version of who she might be, one that incorporated alternative knowledges of life. This version gradually became available to her to enter her life into and to live by.

As Amy began to articulate and perform this alternative and preferred version of who she was, she took various steps to engage others in her project to reclaim her life. These steps were encouraged by my observation that "fieldwork" was an integral part of any such project. I had asked Amy to identify who, of all those persons who had known her, might be the least inaccessible to this new view of who she was[5]. She decided to begin by re-introducing herself to those who were "far away", and contacted several school friends whom she had not seen for several years. Experiencing success in this, she moved to her more immediate social network, which included members of her family of origin, whom she began to invite along to the therapy session. Within the therapeutic context, these family members contributed significantly to the acknowledgement of, and the authentication of, Amy's preferred claims about her life, and to Amy's ability to separate her life from anorexia nervosa.

Anne and John

John and Anne, a separating couple, sought therapy in an attempt to resolve their intense conflict over custody and access in relation to their children, and over property settlement. At the outset of the first meeting, they entered into a fierce dispute, each presenting various claims and counter claims, and only occasionally glancing furtively in my direction. After a time, I interrupted, thanking them both for being so open about the problems they were having with each other, and for providing such a clear demonstration of how things go for them.

After a pause, John and Anne launched into a fresh round of accusations. Fortunately, I was again able to interrupt, explaining that I believed I had a reasonable understanding of their experience of the relationship, and informing them that further demonstrations of this would be unnecessary. Two further such interruptions were necessary before the couple seemed convinced of this.

In the breathing space that followed, I asked to what extent this pattern of interacting - the adversarial one that they had just so clearly demonstrated - was dominating of their relationship; How was this adversarial pattern influencing their perceptions of each other and of their relationship? And how were these perceptions of each other and of their relationship influencing their responses to each other? What did this adversarial pattern have them doing to each other that might be against their better judgement?

After reviewing, with Anne and John, the extent to which this adversarial pattern had been dictating the terms of their relationship, I asked them if this had become their preferred way of responding to each other. Did they find this adversarial pattern captivating? Did this way of being with each other suit them best? Was this adversarial pattern of relating to each other tailor-made for them? Did they experience this way of being together as enriching of their lives?

Both claimed that this was not their preferred way of relating to the other, and both couldn't resist adding that it did seem the preference of the other partner. Since John and Anne claimed that this was not their preferred way of going about things, I suggested that it was unlikely that they had invented it for themselves.

I then encouraged Anne and John to help me understand how they had been recruited into this pattern of responding to differences of opinion over particular issues, and to identify the history of this pattern. Where had they witnessed this pattern before? How were they originally introduced to these techniques for dealing with each other, and what situations first exposed them to these techniques? In what contexts would they expect to find these patterns commonplace, and what justifications are referred to most frequently in order to sustain them? How were they encouraged to subject their relationship to these patterns, to live their relationship out through these patterns?

During this discussion, as John and Anne articulated their experience of this adversarial pattern, it became apparent to them that their relationship was no longer at one with this pattern - they were able to think otherwise about their relationship. I asked them if they were prepared to leave what was left of their relationship to the designs of these patterns, or if they would prefer to intervene and have more to say about the direction of events - to determine a design for what was left of their relationship that would suit them both? In response to this question, John and Anne said that the adversarial pattern was impoverishing their lives, and both indicated that they wanted to free themselves from its dictates.

We then worked to determine what basis there was for an attempt to retrieve what was left of their relationship, and managed to identify several interactions that had not been dominated by the adversarial pattern. One of these related to the extent to which they had been able to evade this pattern for a good part of the interview. Did Anne and John find these interactions with each other more satisfying? Were they at all enthusiastic about these developments? Or were they more attracted to their more familiar ways of being with each other?

As they determined that they were more attracted to this alternative way of interacting with each other, I asked John and Anne what they thought this way of being together had going for it, and why they thought it would suit them to extend these developments. Following this I introduced questions that encouraged them to historicize these more positive developments in their relationship. In responding to these questions, Anne and John recalled a couple that they had befriended early in their marriage. This couple had witnessed several occasions upon which they had been able to resolve a dispute satisfactorily and equitably. A review of this other couple's experience of John and Anne's relationship led to the resurrection of historically situated problem solving knowledges, and, although not without hitches, these became available to them to resolve their disputes over custody, access and property.

Robert

Robert was referred for therapy over abusive behaviour in relation to his partner, and in relation to one of his children. This abuse had only been recently disclosed. He had agreed to leave the family home, and the appropriate police and court measures were in the process of being instituted.

During our early contact, discussion centered on Robert's responsibility for perpetrating the abuse[6], on the identification of the survivors' experiences of abuse, on the real short-term and possible long-term traumatic effects of this on the life of the survivors, and on determining what he might do to take responsibility to mend what might be mended.

Following this work, I asked Robert whether he would be prepared to join me in some speculation about the conditions and the character of men's abusive behaviour. This he agreed to do, so I asked him a series of

questions within the category of those represented below:
- If a man wanted to control and to dominate another person, what sort of structures and conditions could he arrange that would make this possible?
- If a man desired to dominate another person, particularly a woman or a child, what sort of attitudes would be necessary in order to justify this?
- If a man decided to make someone their captive, particularly a woman or a child, what sort of strategies and techniques of power would make this feasible?

During this speculation, particular knowledges about men's ways of being that are subjugating of others were articulated, techniques and strategies that men could rely upon to institute this subjugation were identified, and various structures and conditions that support abusive behaviour were reviewed. I then asked Robert to determine which of these attitudes he had given his life to, which of these strategies had been dominant in shaping his relationships with others, and which of these conditions and structures had provided the framework for his life. This was followed by further discussion centered on a review of the historical processes through which Robert had been recruited into the life space that was fabricated of these attitudes, techniques and structures.

Robert was invited to take a position on these attitudes, strategies and structures. Would he continue to subject his life to this particular knowledge of men's way of being? To what extent did he think it was reasonable to live life as "power's instrument", as an instrument of terror? To what extent did he wish to cooperate with these strategies and tactics that so devastated the lives of others? In view of his developing understanding of the real effects of his actions, did he think it acceptable to depend upon these structures and conditions as a framework for his life?

As this work progressed, Robert began to experience a separation from these attitudes, and an alienation from these structures and techniques of power and control. His previously familiar and taken-for-granted ways of being in relation to women and children, and for that matter, his previously familiar and taken-for-granted ways of being with other men, no longer spoke to him of the truth of who he was as a man. For Robert to challenge his abusive behaviour no longer meant taking action against his own "nature", and he was now able to take entire responsibility for the abuse that he had perpetrated on others.

In the space that Robert stepped into as a result of this separation, we were able to find various unique outcomes; occasions upon which his behaviour had not been compelled by those previously familiar and taken-for-granted ways of being as a man. I asked Robert to evaluate these unique outcomes - did he see these outcomes as desirable? Did he feel positively about them? Or were they of no consequence to him? As Robert concluded that these outcomes were desirable, I asked him to share with me how he had reached this conclusion.

As our work progressed, the identification of these unique outcomes provided a point of entry for an "archeology" of alternative and preferred knowledges of men's ways of being, knowledges that Robert began to enter his live into. For example, in response to my encouragement to give meaning to these unique outcomes, to determine what ways of "being" as a man were reflected in them, Robert recalled an uncle who was quite unlike other men in his family; this was a man who was certainly compassionate and non-abusive. Robert subsequently did some homework on this uncle, and this contributed significantly to his knowledge of some of the more intimate particularities of this alternative way of being.

Robert's family had signalled a strong desire to explore the possibilities of reuniting[7]. As Robert had begun to separate from those attitudes and practices that had justified and supported his abusive behaviour, and as he had entered into an exploration of alternative and preferred knowledges of men's ways of being, the time seemed right to convene a meeting with the family[8]. Understanding his responsibility to provide safeguards to family members, he agreed to participate in certain structures that would contribute significantly to the security of family members. These included (a) a meeting with representatives[9] of his partner and his child to disclose his responsibility for and the nature of the abuse, (b) weekly escape from secrecy meetings[10, 11] with his family and the nominated representatives, and (c) co-operation with other family members in the development of a contingency plan should any family member again feel threatened by abuse.

Over time, Robert traded a neglectful and strategic life for one that he, and others, considered to be caring, open and direct.

An Interview With A Family

The interview had reached a point at which the therapist decided that it was time to hear from the team-members who had been observing the interview from behind a one-way screen. The therapist and the family traded places with the team-members; it was now their turn to be an audience to the team-members' reflections. The team-members first introduced themselves to the family. They then proceeded to share their responses to what family members had judged, or had seemed attracted to, as preferred developments in their lives and relationships.

It was the team members' task to relate to these preferred developments as one might relate to a mystery, a mystery that only family members could unravel. Initially, each observation from a team-member was followed by questions that might encourage family members to account for these developments, and questions that might engage them in speculation about what these developments might mean. Team-members also addressed questions to each other about these developments, inviting further speculation about them. In this way, the family members' fascination in relation to previously neglected aspects of their lived experience was engaged, and they were provoked to enlist their "knowledgeableness" in regard to their own lives.

Some team-members then began to ask other team-members about why they found a particular development interesting. These questions encouraged team members to situate their reflections within the context of their personal experience and their imagination. Team members then invited each other to make transparent what they understood to be the intentions behind their reflections.

Following this, the family and the team again traded places, and the therapist proceeded to interview family members about their experience of the team's reflections; about what comments and questions family members found to be of interest and to the point, and about what comments and questions were not so. As family members began to relate those comments and questions that caught their interest, the therapist asked them to help her understand why they found these interesting, and what realizations and/or conclusions accompanied these comments and questions. The therapist then encouraged family members' speculative assessment about how these realizations and conclusions could affect their

Experience, Contradiction, Narrative & Imagination

day-to-day lives.

The therapist brought the interview to a close by inviting family members and the reflecting team to interview her about the interview, so that she might situate her comments and questions within the context of her own personal experience, imagination and purposes.

DECONSTRUCTION

These stories about therapy portray a number of recurrent practices. I believe that most of these practices relate to what could be referred to as a "deconstructive method", which will be explicated in the following discussion.

I should preface this discussion of deconstruction with an admission - I am not an academic, but, for the want of a better word, a therapist. It is my view that not being situated in the academic world allows me certain liberties, including the freedom to break some rules - for example, to use the term deconstruction in a way that may not be in accord with its strict Derridian sense - and to refer to writers who may not generally be considered to be proposing a deconstructivist method.

According to my rather loose definition, deconstruction has to do with procedures that subvert taken-for-granted realities and practices; those so-called "truths" that are split off from the conditions and the context of their production, those disembodied ways of speaking that hide their biases and prejudices, and those familiar practices of self and of relationship that are subjugating of persons' lives. Many of the methods of deconstruction render strange these familiar and everyday taken-for-granted realities and practices by objectifying them. In this sense, the methods of deconstruction are methods that "exoticize the domestic".

The sociologist who chooses to study his [sic] own world in its nearest and most familiar aspects should not, as the ethnologist would, domesticate the exotic, but, if I may venture the expression, exoticize the domestic, through a break with his [sic] initial relation of intimacy with modes of life and thought which remain opaque to him [sic] because they are too familiar. In fact the movement towards the originary, and the ordinary, world should be the culmination of a movement toward alien and extraordinary worlds.
(Bourdieu 1988, pp.xi-xii)

According to Bourdieu, exoticizing the domestic through the objectification of a familiar and taken-for-granted world facilitates the "reappropriation" of the self. In referring to the reappropriation of the self, I do not believe that he is proposing an essentialist view of self - that in this re-appropriation persons will "find" themselves. Rather, he is suggesting that through the objectification of a familiar world, we might become more aware of the extent to which certain "modes of life and thought" shape our existence, and that we might then be in a position to choose to live by other "modes of life and thought".

If Bourdieu's work can be considered deconstructive, then it is so in a specific sense. His primary interest is in the extent to which a person's situation in a social structure - for example, in academia - is constituting of that person's stance on issues in life.

However, we can also consider deconstruction in other senses: for example, the deconstruction of self-narrative and the dominant cultural knowledges that persons live by; the deconstruction of practices of self and of relationship that are dominantly cultural; and the deconstruction of the discursive practices of our culture.

Deconstruction is premised on what is generally referred to as a "critical constructivist", or, as I would prefer, a "constitutionalist" perspective on the world. From this perspective, it is proposed that persons' lives are shaped by the meaning that they ascribe to their experience, by their situation in social structures, and by the language practices and cultural practices of self and of relationship that these lives are recruited into. This constitutionalist perspective is at variance with the dominant structuralist (behaviour reflects the structure of the mind) and functionalist (behaviour serves a purpose for the system) perspectives of the world of psychotherapy.

In the following discussion, I will consider first the deconstruction of narrative, second, the deconstruction of modern practices of power, and third, the deconstruction of discursive practices. However, I believe, with Michel Foucault (1980), that a domain of knowledge is a domain of power, and that a domain of power is a domain of knowledge. Thus, inasmuch as meaning relates to knowledge, and inasmuch as practices relate to power, I believe that meaning, structures and practices are inseparable in their constitutive aspects.

NARRATIVE

Meaning

The idea that it is the meaning which persons attribute to their experience that is constitutive of those persons' lives has encouraged social scientists to explore the nature of the frames that facilitate the interpretation of experience. Many of these social scientists have proposed that it is the narrative or story that provides the primary frame for this interpretation, for the activity of meaning-making; that it is through the narratives or the stories that persons have about their own lives and the lives of others that they make sense of their experience. Not only do these stories determine the meaning that persons give to experience, it is argued, but these stories also largely determine which aspects of experience persons select out for expression. And, as well, inasmuch as action is prefigured on meaning-making, these stories determine real effects in terms of the shaping of persons' lives.

This perspective should not be confused with that which proposes that stories function as a reflection of life or as a mirror for life. Instead, the narrative metaphor proposes that persons live their lives by stories - that these stories are shaping of life, and that they have real, not imagined, effects - and that these stories provide the structure of life.

In the family therapy literature there are many examples of the conflating of the narrative metaphor and of various conversation/linguistic metaphors. As these metaphors are situated in distinctly different traditions of thought, and as some are at variance with others, I will here present some further thoughts about the narrative metaphor that I hope will adequately distinguish it.

Narrative Structure

Bruner (1986), in referring to texts, proposed that stories are composed of dual landscapes - a "landscape of action" and a "landscape of consciousness". The landscape of action is constituted of (a) events that are linked together in (b) particular sequences through the (c) temporal dimension - through past, present and future - and according to (d) specific plots. In a text, the landscape of action provides the reader with a perspective on the thematic unfolding of events across time.

The landscape of consciousness is significantly constituted by the interpretations of the characters in the story, and also by those of the reader as s/he enters, at the invitation of the writer, the consciousness of these characters. The landscape of consciousness features the meanings derived by characters and readers through "reflection" on the events and plots as they unfold through the landscape of action. Perceptions, thoughts, speculation, realizations and conclusions dominate this landscape, and many of these relate to:

(a) the determination of the desires and the preferences of the characters,
(b) the identification of their personal and relationship characteristics and qualities,
(c) the clarification of their intentional states - for example, their motives and their purposes - and, to
(d) the substantiation of the beliefs of these characters.

As these desires, qualities, intentional states and beliefs become sufficiently elaborated through the text, they coalesce into "commitments" that determine particular careers in life - "life-styles".

If we assume that there is an identity between the structure of texts and the structure of the stories or narratives that persons live by, and if we take as our interest the constitution of lives through stories, we might then consider the details of how persons live their lives through landscapes of action and landscapes of consciousness.

Determinacy

What is the origin of these stories or narratives that are constitutive of persons' lives? The stories that persons live by are rarely, if ever, "radically" constructed - it is not a matter of them being made-up, "out of the blue", so to speak. Our culturally available and appropriate stories about personhood and about relationship have been historically constructed and negotiated in communities of persons, and within the context of social structures and institutions. Inevitably, there is a canonical dimension to the stories that persons live by.

Thus, these stories are inevitably framed by our dominant cultural knowledges. These knowledges are not about discoveries regarding the "nature" of persons and of relationships, but are constructed knowledges that are specifying of a particular strain of personhood and of relationship. For example, in regard to dominant knowledges of personhood, in the West these establish a highly individual and gender distinct specification for ways of being in the world.

Indeterminacy Within Determinacy

If it is the case that the stories that persons have about their lives circumscribe the meanings that they give to experience, as well as the aspects of experience that they select out for expression, and if it is the case that these meanings have particular and real effects in persons' lives, then we have a strong argument for determinacy. And this argument for determinacy is strengthened upon consideration of the extent to which such stories are canonical in that they are co-authored within a community of persons, and in that they are historically constructed within the context of specific institutions and social structures.

However, despite the fact that these stories contribute a certain determinacy to life, rarely do they handle all of the contingencies that arise in "life as lived" in anything like an accomplished way. Just as with texts, in reference to life as lived, the stories that persons live by are full of gaps and inconsistencies, and, as well, these stories constantly run up against contradictions. It is the resolution of these gaps, inconsistencies, and contradictions that contributes to a certain indeterminacy of life; it is these gaps, inconsistencies, and contradictions that provoke persons to engage actively in the performance of unique meaning, or, as Bruner (1990) would have it, in "meaning-making".

Thus, when considering the proposition that life is constituted through an ongoing storying and re-storying of experience, we are considering a process of "indeterminacy within determinacy" - or to what Gertz (1986) concludes to be a "copying that originates".

The wrenching question, sour and disabused, that Lionel Trilling somewhere quotes an eighteenth-century aesthetician as asking - "How Comes It that we all start out Originals and end up Copies?" - finds ... an answer that is surprisingly reassuring: it is the copying that originates. (p.380)

THE DECONSTRUCTION OF NARRATIVE

Externalizing Conversations

For the deconstruction of the stories that persons live by, I have proposed the objectification of the problems for which persons seek therapy (for example, White 1984, 1986, 1989; White & Epston 1989). This objectification engages persons in externalizing conversations in relation to that which they find problematic, rather than internalizing conversations. This externalizing conversation generates what might be called a counter-language, or as David Epston has recently proposed, an "anti-language".

These externalizing conversations "exoticize the domestic" in that they encourage persons to identify the private stories and the cultural knowledges that they live by; those stories and knowledges that guide their lives and that speak to them of their identity. These externalizing conversations assist persons to unravel, across time, the constitution of their self and of their relationships. Externalizing conversations are initiated by encouraging persons to provide an account of the effects of the problem on their lives. This can include its effects on their emotional states, familial and peer relationships, social and work spheres etc, and with a special emphasis on how it has affected their "view" of themselves and of their relationships. Then, persons are invited to map the influence that these views or perceptions have on their lives, including on their interactions with others. This is often followed by some investigation of how persons have been recruited into these views.

As persons become engaged in these externalizing conversations, their private stories cease to speak to them of their identity and of the truth of their relationships - these private stories are no longer transfixing of their lives. Persons experience a separation from, and an alienation in relation to, these stories. In the space established by this separation, persons are free to explore alternative and preferred knowledges of who they might be; alternative and preferred knowledges into which they might enter their lives.

Unique Outcomes and Alternative Stories

How are these alternative knowledges generated and/or resurrected?

What are the points of entry to these other versions of who persons might be? As persons separate from the dominant or "totalizing" stories that are constitutive of their lives, it becomes more possible for them to orient themselves to aspects of their experience that contradict these knowledges. Such contradictions are ever present, and, as well, they are many and varied. Previously, following Goffman, I have referred to these contradictions as "unique outcomes" (White 1988a, 1989; White & Epston 1989), and it is these that provide a gateway to what we might consider to be the alternative territories of a person's life.

For an event to comprise a unique outcome, it must be qualified as such by the persons to whose life the event relates. Following the identification of events that are candidates for a unique outcome status, it is important that persons be invited to evaluate these events; are these events judged to be significant, or to be irrelevant? Do these events represent preferred out-comes, or do they not? Do persons find these developments appealing? Are persons attracted to some of the new possibilities that might accompany these events? If these events are judged to represent preferred outcomes, then persons can be encouraged to give an account of why they believe this to be the case.

When it is established that particular events qualify as unique outcomes in that they are judged to be both significant and preferred, the therapist can facilitate the generation of and/or resurrection of alternative stories by orienting him/herself to these unique outcomes as one might orient themselves to mysteries. These are mysteries that only persons can unravel as they respond to the therapist's curiosity about them. As persons take up the task of unravelling such mysteries, they immediately engage in story-telling and meaning-making.

To facilitate this process which I have called "re-authoring", the therapist can ask a variety of questions, including those that might be referred to as "landscape of action" questions and "landscape of consciousness" questions[12]. Landscape of action questions encourage persons to situate unique outcomes in sequences of events that unfold across time according to particular plots. Landscape of consciousness questions encourage persons to reflect on and to determine the meaning of those developments that occur in the landscape of action.

Landscape of Action Questions

Landscape of action questions can be referenced to the past, present and future, and are effective in bringing forth alternative landscapes that stretch through these temporal domains. In the following discussion, due to considerations of space, I will focus mainly on those questions that resurrect and generate alternative historical landscapes; questions that are historicizing of "unique outcomes". However, some future oriented landscape of action questions will feature in some of the examples that I give.

Questions that historicize unique outcomes are particularly effective in bringing forth alternative landscapes of action. These questions bridge those preferred developments of the present with the past; they encourage persons to identify the history of unique outcomes by locating them within particular sequences of events that unfold through time. Often, these questions assist persons to plot the history of the alternative landscape of action to the extent that they reach back and predate the landscapes of action of the previously dominant and "problem-saturated" stories that persons have had about their lives.

Landscape of action questions can focus on both the recent history and the more distant history of unique outcomes. Those landscape of action questions that bring forth the recent history of the unique outcome mostly relate to its more immediate circumstances:

- *How did you get yourself ready to take this step? What preparations led up to it?*
- *Just prior to taking this step, did you nearly turn back? If so, how did you stop yourself from doing so?*
- *Looking back from this vantage point, what did you notice yourself doing that might have contributed to this achievement?*
- *Could you give me some background to this? What were the circumstances surrounding this achievement? Did anyone else make a contribution? If so, would you describe this?*
- *What were you thinking at the time? Have you been advising yourself differently? What did you tell yourself that pulled you through on this occasion?*
- *What developments have occurred in other areas of your life that may relate to this? How do you think these developments prepared the way for*

Experience, Contradiction, Narrative & Imagination

you to take these steps?

The therapist can encourage the participation of other persons in this generation/resurrection of alternative and preferred landscapes of action. Including members of the community of persons who have participated historically in the negotiation of, and distribution of, the dominant story of the person's life is particularly helpful. For example, other family members can make particularly significant and authenticating contributions to these alternative landscapes of action:

- *How do you think your parents managed to keep their act together in the face of this crisis?*
- *What have you witnessed Harry doing recently that could throw some light on how he was able to take this step?*
- *What did you see Sally doing leading up to this achievement? How does this contribute to an understanding of how she got ready for it?*
- *Would you describe to me the circumstances surrounding this development in your son's life? Did anyone else contribute to this, and if so, in what way?*

The following questions provide examples of those that bring forth the more distant history of the unique outcome. These invite the identification of events and experiences that have a less immediate relation to the unique outcomes. As with those questions that bring forth the recent history of the unique outcome, it is helpful to engage, as co-authors, members of the community of persons who contributed historically to the negotiation and distribution of the dominant story that is repudiated in this re-authoring process.

- *What can you tell me about your history that would help me to understand how you managed to take this step?*
- *Are you aware of any past achievements that might, in some way, provide the back-drop for this recent development?*
- *What have you witnessed in your life up to now that could have given you at least some hint that this was a possibility for you?*
- *I would like to get a better grasp of this development. What did you notice yourself doing, or thinking, as a younger person, that could have provided some vital clue that this development was on the horizon of your life?*
- *Please think about your son's recent feat and reflect on his life as you have known it. With hindsight, what do you recall him doing that could have foreshadowed this, that could have given you a lead on this?*

- It seems that what Mary and Joe have recently accomplished is a manifestation of some behind the scenes work that they have been doing to retrieve their relationship. Were you aware of any signs that this work was taking place? If so, what were these signs?

These examples provide just some of the options for engaging persons in the generation/resurrection of alternative landscapes of action, and I believe that it is not possible to exhaust the choices for this sort of interaction with persons. For example, questions can be introduced to encourage persons to bring forth the recent history and distant history of those events in history that have foreshadowed the current unique outcomes.

As persons begin to articulate preferred events in these alternative landscapes of action, and as they become more engaged in the arrangement or linking of these events in particular sequences through time, they can be encouraged to explicitly name the alternative plot or the counter-plot that is suggested by this arrangement. The name of the alternative plot or counter-plot is important, for it, among other things, (a) contributes very significantly to a person's sense of their life going forward in preferred ways, (b) makes possible the attribution of meaning to events or experiences that would otherwise be neglected or considered to be of little significance, (c) facilitates the session by session sorting and linking of the events that have taken place between sessions, and (d) provides for persons a sense of knowing what might be the next step in their preferred direction in life.

The alternative plot or counter-plot is often named quite spontaneously in the process of this work. When it is not, the therapist can facilitate this by asking questions that encourage persons to generate descriptions in juxtaposition to the previously dominant plot. Through these questions, persons who have been concerned about "losing their relationship" (previously dominant plot), may determine that these developments in the alternative landscape of action suggest that they are on the path of "reclaiming their relationship" (alternative plot or counter-plot). A person who concludes that "self-neglect" has been highly influential in their life (previously dominant plot), may decide that the developments in the alternative landscape of action reflect that s/he has been engaged in a "self-nurturing project" (alternative plot or counter-plot).

Landscape of Consciousness Questions

Landscape of consciousness questions encourage persons to review the developments as they unfold through the alternative landscape of action[13], and to determine what these might reveal about:
(a) the nature of their preferences and their desires,
(b) the character of various personal and relationship qualities,
(c) the constitution of their intentional states,
(d) the composition of their preferred beliefs, and, lastly,
(c) the nature of their commitments.

Landscape of consciousness questions encourage the articulation and the performance of these alternative preferences, desires, personal and relationship qualities, and intentional states and beliefs, and this culminates in a "re-vision" of personal commitment in life[14]. It is through the performance of meaning in the landscape of consciousness that:

... peoples' beliefs and desires become sufficiently coherent and well organized as to merit being called "commitments" or "ways of life", and such coherences are seen as "dispositions" that characterize persons. (Bruner 1990, p.39)

The following questions provide an example of just some of the forms that landscape of consciousness questions might take. These invite persons to reflect on developments as they have unfolded in both the recent and the more distant history of the landscape of action.

- *Let's reflect for a moment on these recent developments. What new conclusions might you reach about your tastes; about what is appealing to you; about what you are attracted to?*
- *What do these discoveries tell you about what you want for your life?*
- *I understand that you are more aware of the background to this turning point in Mary's life. How does this effect the picture that you have of her as a person?*
- *How would you describe the qualities that you experienced in your relationship at this earlier time, when you managed to support each other in the face of adversity?*
- *What do these developments inform you about what suits you as a person?*
- *In more fully appreciating what went into this achievement, what conclusions might you reach about what Harry intends for his life?*
- *It seems that we are both now more in touch with how you prepared yourself for this step. What does this reveal to you about your motives, or*

about the purposes you have for your life?
- *What does this history of struggle suggest about what Jane believes to be important in life, about what she stands for?*

As persons respond to landscape of action and landscape of consciousness questions, they engage in a reliving of experience, and their lives are "retold". Alternative knowledges of self and of relationships are generated and/or resurrected; alternative modes of life and thought become available for persons to enter into. Throughout this re-authoring dialogue, the therapist plays a central role in challenging any early return to the canonical that would suggest that the unique outcome is self-explanatory.

Experience of Experience Questions

Experience of experience questions (White 1988b) greatly facilitate the re-authoring of lives and relationships, and often they are more generative than those questions that encourage the person to reflect more directly on their life. These questions encourage persons to provide an account of what they believe or imagine to be another person's experience of them. These experience of experience questions:
(a) invite persons to reach back into their stock of lived experience and to express certain aspects that have been forgotten or neglected with the passage of time, and
(b) recruit the imagination of persons in ways that are constitutive of alternative experiences of themselves.

Some examples of these experience of experience questions follow. In the examples, these questions are oriented first to alternative landscapes of action, and second to alternative landscapes of consciousness. In the third place, examples are given of questions that encourage persons to bring forth the "intimate particularities" of future developments in these landscapes of action and landscapes of consciousness.

Of course, these questions are not asked in a barrage-like fashion. Instead, they are raised within the context of dialogue, and each is sensitively attuned to the responses triggered by the previous question.

(a) *If I had been a spectator to your life when you were a younger person, what do you think I might have witnessed you doing then that might help me to understand how you were able to achieve what you have recently*

achieved?
- *What do you think this tells me about what you have wanted for your life, and about what you have been trying for in your life?*
- *How do you think that knowing this has affected my view of you as a person?*
- *What do you think this might reveal to me about what you value most?*
- *If you managed to keep this knowledge about who you are close to you over the next week or two, how would it affect the shape of your life?*

(b) *Of all those persons who have known you, who would be least surprised that you have been able to take this step in challenging the problems influence in your life?*
- *What might they have witnessed you doing, in times past, that would have made it possible for them to predict that you could take such a step at this point in your life?*[15]
- *What do you imagine this told them, at that time, about your capabilities?*
- *What would they have assumed to be your purposes in taking this action at this point in your history?*
- *How do you think this spoke to them of who you are, and about what you believe to be important?*
- *Exactly what actions would you be committing yourself to if you were to more fully embrace this knowledge of who you are?*

(c) *I would like to understand the foundations upon which this achievement rests. Of all those persons who have known you, who would be best placed to supply some details about these foundations?*
- *What clues did this provide them with as to which developments in your life were most desirable to you?*
- *What conclusions might they have reached about your intentions in building up these foundations?*
- *What could this have disclosed to them about the sort of life-style you are more suited to?*
- *If you were to side more strongly with this other view of who you are, and of what your life has been about, what difference would this make to your life on a day-to-day basis?*

These examples serve only as an introduction to some of the options for developing questions that encourage the re-authoring of lives according to preferred stories. Among the many other options is the construction of questions that might bring forth future developments in the landscape of consciousness. These questions encourage a reflection on future events in the alternative landscape of action. For example:

- *If you did witness yourself taking these steps, how might this confirm and extend on this preferred view of who you are as a person?*

These questions can then be followed-up by further landscape of action questions, and so on. For example:

- *And what difference would the confirmation of this view make to how you lived your life?*

Other Structures

In the shaping of suitable questions, it can be helpful for the therapist to refer to other structures in this work, including those derived from anthropology, drama and literature. For example, at times unique outcomes appear to mark turning points for which it is difficult to find any antecedents in distant history. Under these circumstances, persons can be encouraged to plot these unique outcomes into a "rite of passage" frame that structures transitions in life through the stages of separation, liminality, and reincorporation (van Gennep 1960).

Alternatively, under these circumstances, unique outcomes can be plotted into a "social drama" frame that structures transitions in life through the stages of steady state, breach, crisis, redress, and new steady state (Turner 1980).

In regard to the borrowing of structures from literature, as I have discovered that the re-vision of motive that accompanies the resurrection of alternative stories and knowledges is particularly "liberating" for persons, I often refer to Burke's deconstruction of motive as a frame for this work.

We shall use five terms as generating principle of our investigation. They are: Act, Scene, Agent, Agency, Purpose. In a rounded statement about motives, you must have some word that names the act (names what took place, in thought or deed), and another that names the scene (the background of the act, the situation in which it occurred); also, you must indicate what person or kind of person (agent) performed the act, what means or instruments he [sic] used (agency), and the purpose ... any complete statement about motives will offer some kind of answer to these five questions: what was done (act), when or where it was done (scene), who did it (agent), how he [sic] did it (agency), and why (purpose). (Burke 1969, p.xv)

In relating experience of experience questions to alternative and historically situated motives, particular acts, scenes, agents, agency, and purposes, can be brought forth[16]. This contributes "dramatically" to the archaeology of alternative knowledges of personhood and of relationship.

An example of the line of questioning that is informed by this structure follows:

(a) *Okay, so your Aunt Mavis might have been best placed to predict such an achievement. Give me an example of the sort of event, that she witnessed in your life, that would have enabled her to predict this achievement.*
(b) *How might she have described the circumstances of the event?*
(c) *Would she have been aware of others who might have contributed to the event?*
(d) *If she had been asked to describe exactly how this was achieved, what do you imagine she would have said?*
(e) *What would she have construed your purposes to be in making this achievement? What do you think she might have learned about what you intended for your life?*

Discussion

At the risk of labouring the point, I want to emphasize that these landscape of action and landscape of consciousness questions are not simply questions about history. They are questions that historicize the unique outcome. And the re-authoring approach that I am describing here is not simply a process of "pointing out positives". Instead, this approach actively engages persons in unravelling mysteries that the therapist can't solve.

When I am teaching this work, following Bruner (1986), I often suggest to therapists that they envision an arch. The arch is a relatively recent development in history[17], and it owes its extraordinary load bearing performance to a specific and sequential arrangement of wedge-shaped stones. Each of these stones is uniquely placed; each stone owes its position to the particular arrangement of stones on either side of it, and in turn makes possible the particular arrangement of stones on either side of it.

The landscape of action can be represented as an arch. And the unique outcome can be represented as one of the wedge shaped stones, its existence understood to be contingent upon its place in a particular class and sequence of events that unfold through time, while at the same time contributing to the particular arrangements of events, across time, on either side of it. Questions that contextualize unique outcomes contribute significantly to bringing forth details about the unique arrangement of events of which the unique outcome is but a part.

A second arch can be envisaged above the first. The landscape of consciousness can be represented by this, and it interacts back and forth with the first arch, the landscape of action, through reflection.

Perhaps the approach that I have described here on the deconstruction of the stories and knowledges that persons live by is not entirely dissimilar to Derrida's work on the deconstruction of texts (1981)[18]. Derrida's intention was to subvert texts and challenge the privileging of specific knowledges with methods that "deconstruct the opposition ... to overturn the hierarchy at a given moment". He achieved this by developing deconstructive methods that:

(a) brought forth the hidden contradictions in texts, and rendering visible the repressed meanings - the "absent but implied" meanings,
(b) gave prominence to those knowledges "on the other side", those considered to be secondary, derivative and worthless.

PRACTICES OF POWER

A good part of Michel Foucault's work is devoted to the analysis of the "practices of power" through which the modern "subject" is constituted (Foucault 1978, 1984). He traced the history of the "art of the government of persons" from the seventeenth century, and detailed many of the practices of self and practices of relationship that persons are incited to enter their lives into. In that it is through these practices that persons shape their lives according to dominant specifications for being, they can be considered techniques of social control.

Constitutive Power

Foucault's (1980) conception was of a modern power that is constitutive or "positive" in its character and effects, not repressive or "negative"; not a power that is dependent upon prohibitions and restrictions.

Rather than propose that the central mechanism of this modern form of power was containing or restricting, he proposed that its central mechanism was productive - persons' lives are actually constituted or made up through this form of power. According to Foucault, the practices of this form of power permeate and fabricate persons' lives at the deepest levels - including their gestures, desires, bodies, habits etc. - and he likened these practices to a form of "dressage" (Foucault 1979).

Local Politics

Foucault was intent on exposing the operations of power at the micro-level and at the periphery of society: in clinics, prisons, families etc. According to him, it was at these local sites that the practices of power were perfected; that it is because of this that power can have its global effects. And, he argued, it is at these local sites that the workings of power are most evident.

So, for Foucault, this modern system of power was decentered and "taken up", rather than centralized and exercised from the top down. Therefore, he argued that efforts to transform power relations in a society must address these practices of power at the local level - at the level of the every-day, taken-for-granted social practices.

Techniques of Power

In tracing the history of the apparatuses and institutions through which these practices were perfected, Foucault (1979) identifies Bentham's Panopticon as the "ideal" model for this form of power - for the:

> ... *technologies of power, which determine the conduct of individuals and submit them to certain ends or domination, an objectivizing of the subject.* (Foucault 1988, p.18)

I have discussed Foucault's analysis of this model elsewhere (White 1989).

This model establishes a system of power in which:
- the source of power is invisible to those who experience it most intensely,
- persons are isolated in their experience of subjugation,
- persons are subject to the "gaze" and to "normalizing judgement",
- it is impossible for persons to determine when they are the subject of surveillance and scrutiny and when they are not, and therefore must assume this to always be the case,
- persons are incited to perpetually evaluate themselves, to police themselves and to operate on their bodies and souls to forge them as docile,
- power is autonomous to the extent that those participating in the subjugation of others are, in turn, the "instruments" of power.

Foucault's analysis of the Panopticon provides an account of how the mechanisms and the structures of this modern system of power actually recruited persons into collaborating in the subjugation of their own lives and in the objectification of their own bodies; of how they became "willing" participants in the disciplining of, or policing of, their own lives. These mechanisms of this modern system of power recruit persons into what Foucault refers to as the ... *technologies of the self, which permit individuals to effect by their own means or with the help of others a certain number of operations on their own bodies and souls, thoughts, conduct, and way of being, so as to transform themselves in order to attain a certain state of happiness, purity, wisdom, perfection, or immortality.* (1988, p.18)

The Ruse

However, this collaboration is rarely a conscious phenomenon. The workings of this power are disguised or masked because it operates in relation to certain norms that are assigned a "truth" status. This is a power that is exercised in relation to certain knowledges that construct particular truths, and is designed to bring about particular and "correct" outcomes, like a life considered to be "fulfilled", "liberated", "rational", "differentiated", "individuated", "self-possessed", "self-contained", and so on.

The descriptions for these "desired" ways of being are in fact illusionary. According to Foucault, they are all part of a ruse that disguises what is actually taking place - these dominant truths are actually specifying of persons' lives and of relationships; those correct outcomes are particular ways of being that are prescribed ways of being.

So, the practices of modern power, as detailed by Foucault, are particularly insidious and effective. They incite persons to embrace their own subjugation; to relate to their own lives through techniques of power that are moulding of these lives, including their bodies and their gestures, according to certain "truths". The ways of being informed by these truths are not seen, by these persons, as the effect of power, but instead as the effect of something like fulfillment, of liberation.

Discussion

This analysis of power is difficult for many persons to entertain, for it suggests that many of the aspects of our individual modes of behaviour that we assume to be an expression of our free will, or that we assume to be transgressive, are not what they might at first appear. In fact, this analysis would suggest that many of our modes of behaviour reflect our collaboration in the control or the policing of our own lives, as well as the lives of others; our collusion in the specification of lives according to the dominant knowledges of our culture.

In undertaking his analysis of the "technologies of power" and the "technologies of the self", Foucault was not proposing that these were the only faces of power. In fact, in relation to fields of power, he proposed the study of four technologies: technologies of production, technologies of sign systems, technologies of power, and technologies of the self (Foucault 1988).

Although I have followed Foucault in emphasizing the techniques of a modern "positive" system of power in this paper, I believe that other analyses of power, including those that relate to Bourdieu's thoughts about the structure of social systems of power and the constitutive effects of these structures on persons' stances in life, are highly relevant in the consideration of the everyday situations that are confronted by therapists.

Other considerations of fields of power would include the extent to which some of the structures that represent the earlier system of sovereign power still exist, and the extent to which institutional inequalities - those of a structural nature and those that relate to an inequality of opportunities - dominate our culture.

In fact, in his analysis of Bentham's Panopticon, Foucault draws attention to a structure that is at the heart of its operations. Upon considering the implications of this structure in terms of inequality, I have elsewhere suggested that, in our culture, men are more often likely to be the "instruments" of the normalizing gaze, and women more often likely to be the subject of this gaze (White 1989). This point has also been made by other authors (e.g. Hare-Mustin 1990).

THE DECONSTRUCTION OF PRACTICES OF POWER

In therapy, the objectification of these familiar and taken-for-granted practices of power contributes very significantly to their deconstruction. This is achieved by engaging persons in externalizing conversations about these practices. As these practices of power are unmasked, it becomes possible for persons to take a position on them, and to counter the influence of these practices in their lives and relationships.

These externalizing conversations are initiated by encouraging persons to provide an account of the effects of these practices in their lives. In these conversations, special emphasis is given to what these practices have dictated to persons about their relationship with their own self, and about their relationships with others.

It is through these externalizing conversations that persons are able to:

(a) appreciate the degree to which these practices are constituting of their own lives as well as the lives of others,
(b) identify those practices of self and of relationship that might be judged as impoverishing of their lives, as well as the lives of others,
(c) acknowledge the extent to which they have been recruited into the policing of their own lives and, as well, the nature of their participation in the policing of the lives of others, and to
(d) explore the nature of local, relational politics.

It is through these externalizing conversations that persons no longer experience these practices as representative of authentic ways of being with themselves and with others. They no longer experience being at one with these practices, and begin to sense a certain alienation in relation to them.

Persons are then in a position to develop alternative and preferred practices of self and of relationship - counter-practices. In therapy, I have participated with persons in challenging various practices of power, including those that relate to:

(a) the technologies of the self - the subjugation of self through the discipline of bodies, souls, thoughts, and conduct according to specified ways of being (including the various operations that are shaping of bodies according to the gender specific knowledges),

(b) the technologies of power - the subjugation of others through techniques such as isolation and surveillance, and through perpetual evaluation and comparison.

And I have also participated with persons in the deconstruction of particular modes of life and thought by reviewing, with them, the constitutive effects of the specific situation of their lives in those fields of power that take the form of social structures. In response to this, persons are able to challenge these effects, as well as those structures that are considered to be inequitable.

Examples

Perhaps it would be timely to return briefly to the stories about Amy and Robert. Amy had been recruited into certain practices of the government of the self - "technologies of the self". She had embraced these practices as a form of self-control, and as essential to the transformation of her life into an acceptable shape - one which spoke to her of fulfillment. She had construed her participation in activities in the subjugation of her own life as liberating activities.

Upon engaging Amy in an externalizing conversation about anorexia nervosa through the exploration of its real effects in her life, she began to identify the various practices of self-government - of the disciplines of the body - and the specifications for self that were embodied in anorexia nervosa. Anorexia was no longer her saviour. The ruse was exposed, and the practices of power were unmasked. Instead of continuing to embrace these practices of the self, Amy experienced alienation in relation to them. Anorexia nervosa no longer spoke to her of her identity. This opened up space for Amy to enter into activities that further subverted the realities constructed by anorexia nervosa, and into an exploration of alternative and preferred practices of self and of relationship.

To Robert, the unexamined and unquestioned knowledges, practices or "technologies of power", structures and conditions that provided the context for his abusive behaviour were all part of a taken-for-granted mode of life and thought that he had considered to be reflective of the natural order of things. Upon entering an externalizing conversation about these knowledges, practices, structures and conditions, and in mapping the real effects of these upon his own life and upon the lives of others, he experienced a separation from this mode of life and thought - this no longer spoke to him of the "nature" of men's ways of being with women and children.

Then, via a unique outcome as a point of entry, Robert was able to engage in an "archeology" of, and the performance of, alternative and preferred practices of relationship. As well, he began to challenge the structures and conditions that are supportive of men's abusive behaviour.

KNOWLEDGE PRACTICES

The professional disciplines have been successful in the development of language practices and techniques that determine that it is those disciplines that have access to the "truth" of the world. These techniques encourage persons in the belief that the members of these disciplines have access to an objective and unbiased account of reality, and of human nature[19].

> *What this means is that certain speakers, those with training in certain special techniques - supposedly to do with the powers of the mind to make contact with reality - are privileged to speak with authority beyond the range of their personal experience.* (Parker & Shotter 1990, p.7)

These language practices introduce ways of speaking and of writing that are considered to be rational, neutral and respectable, emphasizing notions of the authoritative account and the impersonal expert view. These practices disembody the perspective and the opinions of the speaker and the writer. The presentation of the knowledges of the speaker and writer is devoid of information that might give the respondent or the reader information about the conditions of the production of the expert view.

These practices of speaking and writing establish accounts of knowledges that are considered to be "global and unitary" (Foucault 1980), accounts that mask the historical struggles associated with their ascendancy, including the multiplicity of resistances to them. It is difficult for persons to challenge these global and unitary knowledges because the language practices that constitute them include built-in injunctions against questions that might be raised about their socio/political/historical contexts.

Without this critical information, respondents/readers experience a certain "suspension". They do not have the information necessary to determine how they might "take" the views that are expressed, and this dramatically reduces the range of possible responses available to them. Respondents/readers can either subject themselves to the expert knowledge, or they can rail against it. Dialogue over different points of view is impossible.

For the members of the professional disciplines who are operating under the apprehension that they have recourse to objective knowledge, critical reflection on their position is not an option. Thus they are able to avoid facing the moral and ethical implications of their knowledge practices.

A description which contains no critical reflection on the position from which it is articulated can have no other principle than the interests associated with the unanalysed relation that the researcher has with this object. (Bourdieu 1988, p.15)

The open, vague, temporary and changing nature of the world is rendered, by these truth discourses, closed, certain, fixed and permanent. Other ways of speaking/writing are rendered invisible, or, as they are considered to be inferior, are mostly excluded. These "inferior" ways of speaking/writing are only acknowledged if accompanied by the "appropriate" deference to the warranted ways of speaking/writing.

THE DECONSTRUCTION OF KNOWLEDGE PRACTICES

Therapists can contribute to the deconstruction of expert knowledge by considering themselves to be "co-authors" of alternative and preferred knowledges and practices, and through a concerted effort to establish a context in which the persons who seek therapy are privileged as the primary authors of these knowledges and practices. Some of the "therapeutic" practices that are informed by this perspective follow. These by no means exhaust the possibilities, and David Epston and I have discussed other such therapeutic practices elsewhere (e.g. White & Epston 1989; Epston & White 1991).

Therapists can undermine the idea that they have privileged access to the truth by consistently encouraging persons to assist them in the quest for understanding. This can be achieved by giving persons notice of the extent to which the therapist's participation in therapy is dependent upon feedback from persons about their experience of the therapy. It is acknowledged that the person's experiences of therapy is essential to the guidance of the therapy, as this is the only way that a therapist can know what sort of therapeutic interaction is helpful and what is not.

This can be further emphasized if therapists engage persons in some inquiry as to why certain of the ideas that emerge during the interview interest those persons more than other ideas. What is it that persons find significant or helpful about the particular perspectives, realizations, conclusions etc? What preferred outcomes, for persons' lives, might accompany the particular perspectives, realizations, conclusions etc?

Therapists can challenge the idea that they have an expert view by continually encouraging persons to evaluate the real effects of the therapy in their lives and relationships, and to determine for themselves to what extent these effects are preferred effects and to what extent they are not. The feedback that arises from this evaluation assists therapists to squarely face the moral and ethical implications of their practices.

The therapist can call into question the idea that s/he possesses an objective and unbiased account of reality, and undermine the possibility that persons will be subject to the imposition of ideas, by encouraging persons to interview her/him about the interview. In response to this, the therapist is able to deconstruct and thus embody her/his responses (including questions, comments, thoughts, and opinions) by situating these in the context of his/her personal experiences, imagination, and intentional states. This can be described as a condition of "transparency"[20] in the therapeutic system, and it contributes to a context in which persons are more able to decide, for themselves, how they might take these therapist responses.

If the therapist is working with a reflecting team[21], at the end of the session this team can join with persons in interviewing the therapist about the interview. Apart from asking questions about the particular responses of the therapist, at this time team members can be invited to explore the therapist's thoughts about the actual process of the therapy across the interview.

The therapeutic practices of deconstruction and embodiment also hold for the responses of reflecting teams. Reflecting team members can be discouraged from engaging in the time-honoured structuralist and functionalist truth discourses of the psychotherapies, and encouraged to respond to those developments that are identified by family members as preferred developments, or to speculate about those developments that might be preferred [22]. Following this, reflecting team members can interview each other about their reflections so that they might situate these in the context of their personal experience, imagination and intentional states. The options and choices available to persons is maximized through this personalizing of the knowledges of the members of the reflecting team.

The deconstruction of the responses of the members of the reflecting team can be structured around questions like: What was it that caught your attention? Why do you think this caught your attention so? Why did this strike you as so significant? How did you decide to comment on this here? What effect did you think this comment would have?[23] What was your intention in asking this question here?

This transparency of practice provides a challenge to the commonly accepted idea that for therapy to have its desired effects its workings need to be kept secret; the idea that if persons know what the therapist is up to then it won't work. On reviewing these practices with persons, I have learned that they often regard the embodiment of the therapist's and reflecting team's responses to be a highly significant factor in achieving the changes in their lives that they have valued most.

CONCLUSION

Those therapeutic practices that I refer to as "deconstructive" assist in establishing, for persons, a sense of "agency". This sense is derived from the experience of escaping "passengerhood" in life, and from the sense of being able to play an active role in the shaping of one's own life - of possessing the capacity to influence developments in one's life according to one's purposes and to the extent of bringing about preferred outcomes. This sense of personal agency is established through the development of some awareness of the degree to which certain modes of life and thought shape our existence, and through the experience of some choice in relation to the modes of life and thought that we might live by.

Those therapeutic practices that I refer to as deconstructive assist persons to separate from those modes of life and thought that they judge to be impoverishing their own lives and of the lives of others. And they provoke in therapists, and in the persons who seek therapy, a curiosity in regard to those alternative versions of who these persons might be. This is not just any curiosity. It is a curiosity about how things might be otherwise, a curiosity about that which falls outside of the totalizing stories that persons have about their lives, and outside of those dominant practices of self and of relationship.

An emphasis on curiosity in therapeutic practices is by no means new, and I would refer you to Gianfranco Cecchin's (1990) recasting of neutrality. I will leave you with one of Michel Foucault's delightful contributions on this subject:

> *Curiosity is a vice that has been stigmatized in turn by Christianity, by philosophy, and even by a certain conception of science. Curiosity, futility. The word, however, pleases me. To me it suggests something altogether different: it evokes "concern"; it evokes the care one takes for what exists and could exist; a readiness to find strange and singular what surrounds us; a certain relentlessness to break up our familiarities and to regard otherwise the same things; a fervor to grasp what is happening and what passes; a casualness in regard to the traditional hierarchies of the important and the essential.* (1989, p.198)

NOTES

1. I prefer the description "sole parent" over the description "single parent". In our culture, it appears that "single" has so many negative connotations, including of incompleteness, of being unmarried, of failure - of not having made the grade. However, at least to my mind, the word "sole" conjures up something entirely different. It carries a recognition of the extraordinary responsibility that these parents face and of the strength

necessary to achieve what they achieve. And, as well, a second meaning is not hard to discern - "soul". Soul is about essence, and for persons to refer to themselves as "soul parents" is for them to recognise the "heartfulness" that they provide, that their children depend upon to "see them through".

2. The work undertaken here did include exploration of the possibility that the children may have been abused by their father. The findings disconfirmed this as a possibility.

3. In part, this work is premised on the narrative metaphor which brings with it a specific non-essentialist account of authenticity. According to this metaphor, ordinarily a person achieves a sense of authenticity when (a) they perform particular claims about their lives, claims that relate to particular self-narratives, and when (b) this performance is witnessed by themselves or/and others. This would suggest that there is a range of possible authenticities that persons might experience, and that this range is determined by the available stock of stories that persons have about their lives.

4. David Epston, of Auckland, New Zealand, has joined with a number of persons who have sought therapy for anorexia nervosa, in establishing the "The Anti-Anorexia League". The aims of this league are to unmask the "voice" of anorexia nervosa, and to identify, document, and circulate knowledges and practices that are counter to those knowledges and practices upon which the anorexia nervosa depends.

5. Initial steps in fieldwork should not be overly ambitious. Questions like this contribute to more humble beginnings and to increased possibilities in terms of the circulation and the authentication of alternative knowledges of self.

6. I would refer readers to Alan Jenkin's book, "Invitations to Responsibility" (1990) for an excellent discussion of this and other aspects of work with men who abuse others.

7. The counselling of family members in relation to the abuse and other issues was undertaken concurrently in a different context.

8. I do not believe it is ever sufficient for men to take entire responsibility for perpetrating abuse, to identify the experience of those abused, to get in touch with the short term and possible long term effects of the abuse, to develop a sincere apology, to work on ways of repairing what might be repaired, and to challenge the attitudes that justify such behaviour and the conditions and techniques of power that make abuse possible.
    If that is where it ends, although the man may experience genuine remorse, he is likely to re-offend because he has no other knowledges of men's ways of being to live by. For there to be any semblance of security that this will not occur, I believe that it is essential that these men be engaged in the identification and the performance of alternative knowledges of men's ways of being.

9. These representatives must be nominated by the child and the non-offending

spouse, and they can be relatives who do not have a history of abusive behaviour, or persons known to them in the community.

10. Escape from secrecy meetings are held weekly in the first place, and gradually move to a monthly basis over a period of two years. At each of these meetings, events of the past week or so are reviewed. Events which reflect a reappearance of any of those attitudes, strategies, conditions, and structures that provided the context for past abuse can be identified and challenged.

Different family members take turns at minute-taking for these meetings and in the posting of these minutes to the therapist (frequently with the assistance of the representatives). The family member whose turn it is to take this responsibility is encouraged to append their confidential comments to these minutes. If the therapist does not receive the minutes of a meeting on schedule, s/he immediately follows this up. From time to time the therapist joins these meetings to review progress.

It is not possible to over-emphasise the importance of local accountability in this work. State intervention can be highly effective in bringing about the immediate cessation of abuse, but local accountability structures are essential to the establishment of secure contexts.

11. For an excellent discussion of the significance of secrecy in structuring a context for abuse, I would refer readers to Amanda Kamsler and Lesley Laing's "Putting an end to secrecy" (1990).

12. Elsewhere I have referred to landscape of action questions as "unique account" questions, and to landscape of consciousness questions as "unique redescription" questions (White 1988a).

13. Of course, the order of these questions can be reversed. Developments in the landscape of consciousness can be reviewed for what they might reveal about preferred developments in the landscape action. For example, "What did you see yourself doing that led you to this conclusion about your nature?" "What else have you witnessed yourself doing that reflects this belief?"

14. The re-vision of intentional states is often begun ahead of the introduction of these landscape of consciousness questions with the institution of externalizing conversations in relation to the problem. This is achieved through questions like: "What does this problem have you doing that is against your better judgement/what you intend for your life/what you value/what you believe to be important?"

15. Daphne Hewson of the Macquarie University, Sydney, working from the perspectives of both narrative theory and social-cognitive psychology, has pioneered the development of prediction questions as a means of bringing forth the history of alternative stories (see Hewson 1991).

16. What's in a word? Answer - a world! And I believe that, for therapists, the dramatic terms "act", "scene", "agents", "agency", and "purpose", introduce a different world to that world introduced by the terms "what, where, who, how, and why". The terms act and scene impart a sense of the constructed and thematic nature of the world, the terms agent and agency invoke ideas about specific "contributions" and a "know-how" that is related to intentional states, and the term purpose is suggestive of particular intentional states as explanatory notions.

17. Debra Milinsky of Berkeley, who has a strong interest in the history of such matters, informs me that the Etruscans can be most fairly credited for the development of the modern above-ground arch.

18. To my knowledge, there are a number of family therapists now undertaking a study of Derrida's work, and exploring the implications of his ideas in terms of therapeutic practices. Ron Findlay of St Kilda, Victoria, recently presented some of his thoughts on Derrida and therapy at a meeting at Dulwich Centre.

19. Feminist thinkers recognise these language practices as distinctly patriarchal, and seek to challenge them with an ethic of care, within an emphasis on context. For example, see Carol Gilligan's "In a Different Voice" (1982).

20. When discussing with David Epston how I might best depict this deconstruction of the therapist responses, he suggested the term "transparency".

21. For an introduction to the concept of the reflecting team, see Andersen (1987).

22. As with therapist re-authoring practices, reflecting team members orient themselves to unique outcomes as one might orient themself to mysteries. Thus, when team members make comments on unique outcomes, this is followed by questions and perceptions from within the team that are intended to engage the lived experience and imagination of family members in the unravelling of these mysteries. In this way, family members are privileged as the primary authors of alternative and preferred stories.

23. This question was suggested by Stephen Madigan during his visit to Dulwich Centre through the "Down Under Family Therapy Scholarship".

REFERENCES

Andersen, T. 1987:
    The reflecting team: Dialogue and meta-dialogue in clinical work. **Family Process**, 26:415-428.
Bourdieu, P. 1988:
    Homo Academicus. California; Stanford University Press.

Bruner, J. 1986:
  Actual Minds, Possible Worlds. Cambridge, MA; Harvard University Press.
Bruner, J. 1990:
  Acts of Meaning. Cambridge, Mass; Harvard University Press.
Burke, K. 1969:
  A Grammar of Motives. Berkeley; University of California Press.
Cecchin, G. 1987:
  Hypothesizing, circularity and neutrality revisited: An invitation to curiosity. **Family Process**, 26(4):405-413.
Derrida, J. 1981:
  Positions. Chicago; University of Chicago Press.
Epston, D. & White, M. 1990:
  Consulting your consultants: The documentation of alternative knowledges. **Dulwich Centre Newsletter**, No.4, pp.25-35.
Foucault, M. 1979:
  Discipline and Punish: The birth of the prison. Middlesex; Peregrine.
Foucault, M. 1980:
  Power/Knowledge: Selected interviews and other writings. New York; Pantheon Books.
Foucault, M. 1984:
  The History of Sexuality. Great Britain; Peregrine Books.
Foucault, M. 1988:
  Technologies of the self. In Martin, L., Gutman, H., & Hutton, P. (Eds.), **Technologies of the Self**. Amherst; University of Massachusetts Press.
Foucault, M. 1989:
  Foucault Live. New York; Semiotext(e).
Geertz, C. 1986:
  Making experiences, authoring selves. In Turner, V. & Bruner, E. (Eds.), **The Anthropology of Experience**. Chicago; University of Illinois Press.
Gilligan, C. 1982:
  In a Different Voice. Cambridge, Mass; Harvard University Press.
Hare-Mustin, R. 1990:
  Sex, lies and headaches: The problem is power. In Goodrich, T. (Ed.), **Women and Power: Perspectives for therapy**. New York; W.W.Norton.
Hewson, D., 1991:
  From laboratory to therapy room: Prediction questions for reconstructing the 'new-old' story. **Dulwich Centre Newsletter**, No.3, pp.5-12.
Jenkins, A. 1990:
  Invitations to Responsibility: The therapeutic engagement of men who are violent and abusive. Adelaide; Dulwich Centre Publications.
Kamsler, A. 1990:
  Putting an end to secrecy: Therapy with mothers and children following disclosure of child sexual assault. In Durrant, M. & White, C. (Eds.), **Ideas for Therapy with Sexual Abuse**. Adelaide; Dulwich Centre Publications.

Parker, I. & Shotter, J. (Eds.) 1990:
 Deconstructing Social Psychology. London; Routledge.
Turner, V. 1980:
 Social drama and stories about them. **Critical Inquiry**, Autumn.
van Gennep, A. 1960:
 The Rites of Passage. Chicago; Chicago University Press.
White, M. 1984:
 Pseudo-encopresis: From avalanche to victory, from vicious to virtuous cycles. **Family Systems Medicine**, 2(2):150-160.
White, M. 1986:
 Negative explanation, restraint, and double description: A template for family therapy. **Family Process**, 25(2):169-184.
White, M. 1988a:
 The process of questioning: A therapy of literary merit? **Dulwich Centre Newsletter**, Winter, pp.8-14.
White, M. 1988b:
 Saying hullo again: The incorporation of the lost relationship in the resolution of grief. **Dulwich Centre Newsletter**, Spring, pp.7-11.
White, M. 1989:
 The externalizing of the problem and the re-authoring of lives and relationships. **Dulwich Centre Newsletter**, Summer, pp.3-21.
White, M. & Epston, D. 1989:
 Literate Means to Therapeutic Ends. Adelaide; Dulwich Centre Publications. (Republished as **Narrative Means to Therapeutic Ends**. New York; W.W.Norton.)

CHAPTER VIII

STRANGE AND NOVEL WAYS OF ADDRESSING GUILT

David Epston

Previously published in
Walsh, F. & McGoldrick, M. (Eds)
"Living Beyond Loss: Death in the Family"
New York; W.W.Norton, 1991.

Reprinted in "Family Systems Medicine", 1991, 9(1).
Reprinted in "Revista Sistemas Familiares", 1992 (forthcoming).

Guilt associated with the death or dying of others is well-known, but there has been little discussion of it apart from those conventions derived from the notion of "working through". It is almost as if, in the face of death and dying, the creativity many therapists bring to bear on their work is forsaken. The seriousness adopted can stymie any measures apart from attempting to talk the person out of feeling guilty. I am not arguing here that we should not take death and dying seriously; rather, I am advocating the deep play associated with creative endeavour. The stories that follow are written with the hope that others might be encouraged to play deeply in the face of death and dying, for in the stories of Billy, Hayden, and Martin and Sally, the therapist was required by urgency to have recourse to such an aptitude. In each case study, the person was experiencing guilt somewhere along the continuum of self-accusation/condemnation, self-punishment, self-starvation, self-torture, self-exile, and finally self-execution. For Billy, Hayden, and Martin, rapid and enduring relief was found by strange and novel ways.

BILLY GIVES GUBA THE SLIP

Billy, aged 12, was referred to a residential community because of his persistent truanting, running away from home and, more recently, abusing alcohol. Billy was the third of four sons from a fundamentalist family. His father worked long days in his small business but still had trouble making ends meet and the family's circumstances were impoverished. The mother had come from an "aristocratic" and highly successful family that had rejected her when she married her husband.

At the age of three, Billy had been struck down by a bicyclist, sustaining disfiguring facial injuries that had required corrective surgery. Although this surgery was very successful, from that day on, the family story went, Billy had "rejected" his parents. By their account, Billy refused to accept their attempts to "cuddle" him and commenced wandering away from home. According to Billy, they blamed him for his "stupidity" for running into the path of the cyclist; Billy blamed them, in return, for not having watched over him adequately.

When Billy was seven, his father was diagnosed with cancer of the kidney. The father's condition deteriorated over the next three years. Finally, a last ditch attempt was made to save his life by surgery and, surprisingly, he went into remission for some time.

I was urgently requested to consult with Billy two years after his father's surgery and six weeks after his family insisted on his admission to residential care because of his failure to attend school and the danger posed by his running away. He had attended less than ten days of school in the previous six months. Billy's father's health had suddenly deteriorated drastically and his mother became emotionally paralyzed, refusing to talk to anyone. Because there were no other family members able to care for Billy, residential placement became a way to avoid the legal action that would make him a ward of the state. It would also maximize the possibility that Billy and his family could be reunited at some time in the future.

The family therapy team of the residential unit found Billy's family to be "devastated" and extremely difficult to reach. Meanwhile, the therapeutic community could not contain Billy by recourse to any conventional measures. He continued to run away by night, making his getaway on stolen bicycles. He had stolen 20 by the time I met him. At the same time, he had suffered numerous physical injuries, many of which he really couldn't explain. Both staff and fellow residents felt there was "something crazy about him", and none of them liked associating with him. What was most unnerving for Billy's therapist was the reckless way he rode his stolen bicycles, at times appearing to throw himself into the path of oncoming cars. At other times, he could be found sheltering in churches, perilously perched in the belfries, drunk on altar wine. Once he had broken into the home of a funeral director and stolen the keys to their hearse. These events so distressed the residential staff that the only option they could see to reduce the mayhem he was creating was to transfer him to a secure unit where he could be incarcerated. Instead, the therapist, in an attempt to bring Billy under some measure of control, commenced the ritual process that Michael White (1989) developed called "the ritual of inclusion". This ritual involves a phase of physical restraint but is reframed as a matter of getting in touch with others rather than punishment. Such a ritual process often triggers a crisis of intimacy in which the young person seeks out physical closeness and a sense of belonging.

In the intimacy that this intervention provoked, Billy told his therapist of his conviction that he had caused his father's cancer and was possessed by a devil. Attempts were made to convince him otherwise; when these failed Billy saw his family doctor, whose efforts fared no better. Everyone felt so desperate that someone proposed an exorcism, a practice that was consistent with the family's fundamentalist Christianity. Billy seized this opportunity, which was enacted under the appropriate ecclesiastical guidance. He experienced immediate relief, but, unfortunately, it only endured for 24 hours before he felt his "devil" had regained control over him. It was at this point that I was requested to consult to Billy and his therapist. His father's medical condition had recently deteriorated and his death was believed to be imminent. We speculated that Billy would expect his devil to demand his own death in retribution for his father's demise.

I was requested by the unit's family therapy team to do an emergency consult with Billy. One thing seemed strongly in my favour in meeting him: I am a cyclist and had ridden to the consultation on a racing cycle, wearing a cycling jersey under my shirt. How could two cyclists not join together? When Billy entered the room, I was surprised how open, friendly, and unsuspicious he was. Still, I thought it would be prudent to show my credentials. I asked if he would like to check over my bicycle. He eagerly accepted. I revealed my cycling jersey. My first question, after our "cyclist's union", was, "Have you ever had a good day in your life?" He considered the question very seriously and came up with his answer: "That day in the church when I got exorcized ... and the day I got my first bicycle". As the effects of the former experience were so short-lived, I decided to pursue the latter. I invited him to tell me about it in detail. To assist him in his description, I asked what his bicycle had been called. His answer was fortuitous: "Sidewinder!" I then enquired if he knew what a sidewinder was. "Yes", he said, "a deadly snake". I agreed with him: "You're quite right. No-one in his right mind would mess with a sidewinder". From here on in, I took every opportunity to add the comments - "Cycles are good ... cycling is good ... cyclists are good ... and goodness drives out badness" - into our conversation. These comments located us in the same status: good cyclists opposed to badness. Billy's belief was that he was possessed by the devil and consequently evil-doing had been immune to discrediting. I provided him with a counter-proposition, one that no longer constrained him in blindness to discrepancies between events in his father's life and events in his own.

I then requested that he show me his devil by drawing a picture of it. He did so without any reservation. His representation had horns, a trident, a forked tail, and a third eye in the middle of his forehead. Underneath was inscribed "Guba". I showed no fear but treated Guba's representation with the same degree of respect one would accord any worthy adversary. I placed the picture of Guba in one corner of the room and asked Billy and his therapist to bring their chairs and join me in the opposite corner. We huddled and spoke in confidential and hushed tones. I renamed Billy "Sidewinder". His therapist accepted the name of the "White Knight", and I took the name of the "Avenging Angel". Right there and then, we all agreed to join forces against Guba. Whenever an opportunity arose, I restated the counter-proposition: "Cyclists are good; goodness drives out badness".

I then proceeded to tell Billy about the Molteni cycling jersey that had recently been returned to me by another client, who had had life-threatening asthma. It had been his talisman while he gained good control over his asthma and had become a competent cyclist. I also informed him that the most famous cyclist in the world, Eddie Mercyxx, rode for the Molteni Spaghetti Company and won the Tour de France five times. I then went into some detail how "the Molteni" assisted me in cycling from England to France and said that, when I weakened, I always knew I could count on "the Molteni" to get me to my destination, no matter what. At the end of the session I gave "the Molteni" to Billy.

I started regularly telephoning Billy and would initiate contact as follows: "Come in, Sidewinder ... come in. Can you read me? This is the Avenging Angel ... can you read me?" After Billy would acknowledge our contact, I would enquire: "Any sign of the enemy today? Has Guba tried to bug you or take over your mind?" Billy usually told of some skirmishing and the tactics he was now employing, concluding with, "And I gave Guba the slip". I would check with him if he thought he had enough resources and he would reassure me that "the Molteni" was working. "I'll check back in a few days, Sidewinder. This is the Avenging Angel signing off. Over and out."

We met again two months later after my return from overseas. Billy, according to both himself and his therapist, had utterly repossessed himself. I found it hard to conceal my amazement. Within two weeks of our first meeting, he had stopped running away, stealing bicycles, and damaging himself, and had become more accessible to both his therapist and fellow residents. I asked his permission to ask him a number of questions so I could satisfy my curiosity as to how he had given Guba the slip. The following is the 'letter' format I used to validate Billy's new story by retelling it.

Dear Sidewinder,

This is a copy of our talk today. You can read it over when you want to. If you forget it, this will help you remember it. Billy, this is what you had to say:

    The Molteni jersey made me believe that I could fight Guba. I think Guba didn't like it. He's ready to make another move. But he can be killed by goodness. I'm into goodness and Guba is into badness. My special name gave me strength because it stands for a very poisonous snake. My therapist, Tim, makes sure I'm good and not bad. Tim is on the side of goodness and strength. I didn't know I had so much strength of mind before today. I figured this out when Tim promoted me to a higher grade in the residence. If I keep going, I soon will be a senior. I am getting used to the fact that I have inside of me a personal strength and goodness. I have tons more goodness today than when I first met you. Your friend, Michael White, was right when he said that I would be all right because I could fight back against Guba and that I shouldn't be so impatient. He was right too when he said that everything that needed to be done had been done and that I would do the rest.[1]

    I know that life is full of ups and downs and when I am down, I will be vulnerable to the tricks and sneakiness of Guba. It is easy to fight back, even when I am down and Guba tries to take over my mind again. I have a mind of my own now and it is a strong mind. I can call on the White Knight and the Avenging Angel if Guba tries to make a sneaky move on me. I have already fought back by using my mind strength to be good and not be tricked into doing bad. I just didn't listen to Guba anymore. I just told myself not to listen and that's all there was to it. Even if Guba shouted at me, I could shout even louder. I got my strength from within my own mind and I know now I always had it. The trouble was I didn't know I had it. Now I know.

    I was really interested to learn of your anti-Guba tactics. Still, it might be a very good idea to practice fighting Guba with Tim. How you could do this is by pretending you are down and vulnerable and to spy on the ways Guba tries to ambush your mind and take it over with its garbage. Tim will help you here by helping you pretend and by helping spy on Guba's habits. If Guba is going to fight dirty, you are going to have to be on the look-out. Spying is the best thing to do while life is on the up for you. If the going gets tough, you will be ready for anything Guba tries on you to take over your mind. Guba is going to be awfully upset to find that you have strengthened your mind so much. He usually preys upon weak minds. You are no weakling - that's for sure. Keep this in a safe place. *Yours sincerely, The Avenging Angel.*

Still, fearing for Billy's sanity in the event of his father's death, we thought it prudent to make provisions for this possibility, should our interventions fail. We arranged to meet with Billy's oldest brother, who had just returned from abroad, for a videotaped discussion. We suggested its purpose be the exculpation of Billy, but that we might have to save the video until Billy was ready to appreciate its contents. However, Billy was enthusiastic about viewing the video as the relationship with this brother was his strongest relationship in his family. During my discussion with Billy's brother, I proposed an explanation of the father's cancer to counter Billy's: "Your dad works so hard ... it's almost as if he's working himself to death". Billy's brother agreed and we investigated this proposition at some length during our videotaped meeting. Although I had been informed that Billy's father denied that his life was in danger and had refused to discuss any plans for the family's future with either his wife or Billy's therapist, I wrote him a letter, seeking his co-operation in preparing a video.

Dear Mr Brown,

I am putting my thoughts in writing because I cannot be there when you make the video with Tim [the therapist]. I regret that I am unable to do so. This next hour could be the most critical experience for your son's future. I am aware that this is dramatic, so allow me to explain myself. As you may know, Billy mistakenly believes that he, and he alone, is responsible for your cancer and any suffering you have undergone. Although you may be surprised by this and unwilling to accept his childish beliefs, he entertains these ideas despite your best intentions to dissuade him and our best attempts to talk him out of it. It seems to us that he formed these ideas some years ago when he was very young and from his point of view, everything that has happened since then supports his argument. He cannot yet see it from an adult point of view because to some extent he is stuck at an earlier level in his thinking. His love for you is so great that he is devastated by your illness. If he loved you less, his problem would be considerably smaller and we would not be so concerned. He believes unconsciously that he should be punished and tortured and that is exactly what he does to himself at times. These times are very dangerous for his well-being. There is also a grave risk that he will have a tortured lifestyle, in which his unconscious thoughts of guilt and blame for your suffering will dictate self-punishments to him. If we do not do something, it is possible he will serve a life sentence for something he did not do. He will pay with self-torture for a crime he did not or could not have committed. We know this, you know this, but Billy has a very different set of ideas to explain your misfortunes. He is a victim, like you and your family, but he views himself as your villain.

It is my opinion that you, and only you (as his father and the one who is suffering the most) can absolve him. And I am afraid to say that his suffering may persist until he has the adult understanding to believe your words and be fully aware of their meaning. I request, for your son's sake (and your own), that you record and document your absolution of your son to keep him from torturing himself with guilt and blame for your illness. It is not likely that this will have an immediate impact but we promise you that we will hold it in trust and make it available to Billy when either he or we think he is ready to know the real truth. So no matter what happens to you or us, this tape will remain the property of your son, and I believe that it may very likely mean the difference between a tortured lifestyle for Billy and a good future. Once again, it is my considered opinion that what you are about to do will have more influence over your son's life than anything else, aside from his conception and birth.

I am not there with you and Billy's therapist, but I want you to know I am there in spirit. Good luck to you both and what you do now could change the course of Billy's life.   *Yours with respect and admiration, David*

Billy's father decided against a videotaped meeting but instead chose to meet with Billy himself. Four months later he died. Billy, along with his family, had been at his father's bedside throughout the last week of his life. Although his grief was profound, Billy was able, at all times, to act with personal dignity and integrity and support other family members. At his therapist's suggestion, Billy accompanied his father's body to the crematorium along with his therapist and the minister, and once again participated in every way possible until all there was left for him to do was say farewell to his father.

Two years later I learned that Billy had grown quite a bit and probably could fit into the Molteni. So we arranged to meet together. Billy recalled how Guba "got inside me and caused me to run away and get into bad things ... it instructed my brain to just do things". When I asked how he accounted for his success, he proposed a number of possibilities:

BB: *Firstly, I found out that people did care about me. Before I didn't think anyone cared about me. Secondly, the Molteni. A good friend gave it to me ... and that's you. I knew I would be able to trust it. Like God gave this to you or the person who gave it to you. It was like a powerful thing that would stop all my enemies. And I know that ever since I've had it, it stopped everything bad from happening to me. I really thank it. And thirdly, express your life to people that you know love you ... After I was talking to you, it sort of lost power like when you see electricity in a light and then you turn it off.*

DE: *Now tell me, before Guba was giving you the idea that you were to blame for your father. When your dad died, that would have been a time I would have thought that Guba would have tried to reassert itself in your mind. Did it not have any impact on you? None of these ideas got through to you?*

BB: *No ... no ... I was believing for a while that I was the one to blame for my dad getting sick.*

DE: *How did you get that idea?*

BB: *Guba made a signal into my mind, but I was the one to get out of it. I listened to my father when he talked to me. He told me to try to get better because he knew what was happening to me.*

DE: *You got yourself out of that idea?*

BB: *Yah!*

DE: *If you didn't have the strength you had, what do you think Guba would have done to you in the end?*

BB: *He probably would have turned me into a vegetable and sent me to a psycho hospital.*

DE: *I'm glad that didn't happen.*

BB: *So am I.*

DE: *Because you strike me as a very fine person and if I had to describe you in one word, it would be courageous. It seems to me that you have lived through a pretty hard thing for a young person - your dad's death. And Tim gave me the impression that you were particularly helpful to your family and your father would have been very proud of you. Do you think so?*

BB: *Yes.*

After our discussion, Billy posed for a photograph wearing the

Addressing Guilt

Molteni. I then invited him for an inaugural ride on my bicycle. He returned 15 minutes later, having worked up a good sweat, but he and my bicycle were in one piece. Never I have known anyone to look so proud when he dismounted and returned my helmet. Since then, Billy has become a very popular young person, both in the residence and at school, where he is regarded as "the most centred kid".

Considerable work has been done by the therapeutic team to assist Billy and his mother in reuniting, a very difficult proposition, because after the father died it was discovered that he had mortgaged all his life insurance and the mother had to sell their home to pay off their creditors. In this process, a second son had to move in with friends. (At this point efforts are being made to shore up financial resources and extend family support for Billy's mother to enable the family to come together again. It seems likely that Billy will be able to return to his family in the near future.)[2]

CONFESSION, PENANCE, AND ABSOLUTION[3]

Sally, aged 26, made an appointment for her husband, Martin, aged 28, and herself because her husband was refusing to acknowledge her three-month-long pregnancy. When I met and talked with them, it was very easy to understand why. Sally and Martin had met at age 13 and 15 and had joined their lives together almost from then. They had always wanted children; however, first they travelled abroad so that Martin could advance in his accounting career. This was very important to him because his family had been very poor as a result of his father's unwise business decisions. He, by contrast, wished to ensure the financial security of his family, including his mother, who had separated from his father, and his mother's mother. Sally became pregnant while they were living abroad and wished to return home. Martin urged that they stay on for another year to complete his contract. Because there was some indication of obstetric risk, near the end of her pregnancy Sally was to be admitted for a "trial of labour" to decide whether a caesarian section was indicated. The medical staff mistakenly proceeded with normal birthing. After 18 hours of labour, a young doctor unsuccessfully attempted a high forceps delivery, and Sally was then urgently transferred to the operating room. During the delay, the baby stopped breathing and had to be resuscitated. As a result, he was profoundly brain-damaged. Martin and Sally returned with their baby to New Zealand, and the baby spent nine months between hospital and home before he died. This was an extremely difficult time for all concerned and their distress and grief were almost unendurable.

During this time, Martin became preoccupied with his guilt. He blamed himself on two counts: first, if he hadn't wanted to remain in England this wouldn't have happened, and, second, he should have been aware that the medical staff were mistaken and acted accordingly to set them right. Although Sally acknowledged that she had some grieving to do, she felt able "to look forward rather than backward" and had deeply hoped that the current pregnancy would have the same effect on Martin.

On the contrary, Martin was quite oblivious. Although he was still able to maintain his job, he became preoccupied with all the reasons he was to blame for their first child's demise. This was taking two to three hours of his time every day. In addition, he was preparing a legal action against the doctor in question. He was determined to pursue this course despite what he described as "a hell of a lot of conflict in my mind". To some extent, he didn't know whom to blame more - the doctor or himself.

I listened for quite a while and then asked this question: "How many people have tried to talk you out of your guilt?" They assured me that their many friends and family had done just that without any success whatsoever. In fact, Martin now avoided all social occasions. He described feeling estranged and "not normal". In our discussion, I alternated the more self-referential term "self-torture" for guilt and then used it almost exclusively. I proposed that there was a well-established escape route from self-torture: confession, penance, and absolution. I enquired if they had ever heard of this. They laughed for the first time and assured me they had. I asked once again if they thought there was any chance of my convincing Martin that he oughtn't to feel so guilty, since "after all, it's not your fault". They insisted that this had been tried extensively without Martin's experiencing any relief whatsoever.

So we all agreed to start with Martin's confession. I invited him to employ the "seven deadly sins" as his moral reference point. He was very clear about the charges he had laid against himself:

The reason we were in England was because of my drive ... I kept Sally there by a mixture of deceit and God knows what else ... On the day of the labour, I didn't grab anyone by the hand ... I wish I hadn't been so concerned about Sally. I should have looked at what people were doing.

Sally and I convened and came up with the sins of dishonesty, greed, and ignorance. Martin found himself 100% to blame. Sally and I started to work out some appropriate penance, which we referred to as "torture" instead of "self-torture". We came up with ideas for "torture runs" and "torture jobs", all of which were particularly benevolent, since over the period of time since the baby's death Martin had gained 30 pounds and was extremely overweight. The mood changed dramatically and it would be fair to say that we were all laughing loudly, especially when we would concur with one of Martin's self-charges and also insist that he hadn't fully considered his "sinfulness".

The following letter was sent to them immediately after the session:
Dear Martin and Sally,

You made your confession yesterday, which probably was something of a relief to you. Now you are in a better position to take some affirmative action in the form of penance. This will take the place of self-torture. As you yourself noted, self-torture was a sentence without limit - a life sentence, in fact. There was the possibility that your mind would become your prison and your guilt would become your jailer.

In your confession, you found yourself 100% to blame for the following self-charges:

1. In order to provide for your mother and grandmother and your own family in a manner different from that of your father, you travelled to England to secure a good income. You did this so that you would not experience the insecurities that you did as a child. You were driven because of these concerns to advance yourself in your career and you did everything in your power to convince Sally to stay on. For the above, you have accused yourself of the sins of dishonesty and greed and have found yourself guilty.

2. During the day of Sally's labour, "I didn't grab someone by the hand. I should have looked at what people were doing". Instead, you were guilty of spending all your time by Sally, comforting her and sharing her pain. You have found yourself guilty of ignorance. "I should have known what 'trial of labour' meant, should have gone to medical school and done a post-graduate Diploma of Obstetrics and Gynaecology".

Instead, you advanced yourself in your accounting career and invested a lot of time and energy in it. And, in addition, you refused to work as an accountant for altruistic motives and insisted on payment for your services. With your payment, instead of giving all your money away to a worthy cause - Sally suggested the Society for the Prevention of Cruelty to Animals - you attempted to secure your life and Sally's, along with the generation of your children and the generations of your mother and her mother.

You agreed that justice would only be done if you inflicted upon yourself some fair and just penance for the sins of greed, dishonesty, and ignorance. And I imagine there were a few other deadly sins that slipped your mind during your confession.

The tortures are as follows:

1. Every day, rain or shine - I hope it rains! - you are to rise at the unseemly hour of 6.30am, don appropriate jogger's suit, and run for exactly 20 minutes. During this time, you are to say over and over to yourself a list of the ways you, Martin, can insult yourself. Sally will provide you with such a list and replenish it when required.

2. Sally will allow you to forget to put the rubbish out and then insist that you put it out late at night and do so barefoot.

3. Martin, you are to leave your clothes all over the place and Sally will hide them so you, Martin, will experience a sharp, short burst of torture finding them. Sally will claim that her pregnancy has made her forgetful and that she just can't help herself.

4. Martin, you are to paint the roof within one month's time. Randomly, Sally will phone you so you have to get down from the roof, being the kind of person who can't resist answering the telephone. Sally will enquire if you are torturing yourself to your satisfaction.

5. Once again, during tortures 2, 3 and 4, Martin, you are to recite to yourself your self-blaming jingles that Sally will compose for you.

I look forward to meeting you both in one month's time to see if you, Martin, are ready for absolution. Good luck!   Yours sincerely, David.

We met one month later and, as soon as we saw one another, we all cracked up laughing. Martin informed me that he had "slightly changed your torture" from running to swimming. He was doing between six and eight lengths of the pool per day. I commented, "Swimming is good because you are quite mindless. Did you fill your mind up with blaming?" He laughed and told me he just didn't have the energy for it. Good progress was being made on the roof too. Sally informed me that Martin had become more energetic, more "like your old self" and less depressed. When

I asked when this occurred, she said: "Straightaway really! You were better within 24 hours". Martin happily agreed, saying that he no longer felt "abnormal" and was 80% of his old self: "I'm getting so close that a lot of people wouldn't notice the difference".

DE: *What do you think happened at this place that set the stage for your comeback?*

ML: *It acted like a turning point. Now, whether that turning point would have happened a bit further along, we don't know. But it couldn't have happened when he died. It was a couple of months after and it was a turning point. That's the only way you can describe it.*

DE: *How do you understand how that occurred? What do you think I did or said that allowed all of you to change course in a sense?*

ML: *You were sensible in what you said but the approach you took was slightly silly, bordering on the ridiculous. It was that approach. Underneath, I could see your motives and they were good. It was slightly ridiculous. It made everything I was feeling seem ridiculous.*

SL: (bursting out laughing) *And it was that thing you said that a lot of people have been telling you that it wasn't your fault. And that didn't work. If you're guilty, you've got to get it out of your system.*

We then went on to discuss how they had grown apart by protecting each other by "going off into our little, separate corner". They felt that the wedge that had been driven between them was gone. They also talked about the friction that had arisen between them with Sally encouraging Martin "to become your old, confident self" and Martin feeling annoyed. Sally also expressed her relief that Martin was no longer indifferent to her pregnancy. She had feared that he would, in a manner of speaking, lose this child too. They agreed that this was all behind them, although they still had some grieving to do. Now they were determined to share their grief. Martin had taken up all the social activities he had abandoned. They had carefully selected a "good gynaecologist" and were confident things would go well this time.

I don't think I ever looked forward to a six-month follow-up quite so much. Sally told me that she would be having a caesarian and couldn't wait to have her baby in her arms. Martin was somewhat apprehensive but doing well. She then laughed and told me that I might be interested to learn that Martin was now swimming a kilometre a day and had lost 30 pounds in weight. When I asked what was happening with their legal action, she replied, "You know, Martin hasn't mentioned it since the first time we saw you six months ago". I wished her well.

Three weeks later I received a card announcing the birth of a "beautiful and healthy baby girl". We met a year later for review and for me to meet their daughter. Martin informed me that he now considered that the death of his son had deepened him as a person, and for that he would be forever grateful. Their legal action was proceeding but Martin no longer had any interest in it and was considering withdrawing it.

HAYDEN BARLOW REGAINS HIS APPETITE[4]

Hayden, aged 11, had had a malignancy diagnosed when he was three, and had had several rounds of surgery, radiotherapy, and chemotherapy. Recently there had been a recurrence involving further surgery. This was followed, over a period of several months, by a dramatic weight loss and complete loss of appetite, apparently unrelated to his disease process. I was asked to consult with him and see if I could find out what he thought the problem might be. Hayden pulled the brim of the baseball cap he customarily wore down over his face. All I could see were his tears trickling out from under it. He hated anyone to see him cry. He told me he couldn't eat. Every time he sat down to a meal he would see a drip and feel nauseated, just like he did after chemotherapy. At night he had nightmares of tombstones with drip bottles and infusion lines running into them. He was dying while doctors and nurses climbed out of the tombstones towards him saying, "We're going to get you! It's your fault!" Then he would turn to see a truck bearing down on him. Although Hayden seemed relieved to tell me of his fears, I knew this was insufficient for him to recommence his chemotherapy. Hayden requested that I tell his parents what was happening to him. He had been unable to reveal to them that his usual bravado was just a front. The family agreed to a referral for family therapy.

When I first met Cynthia and Roy Barlow, they appeared both confused and desperate. Hayden was buried beneath his baseball cap and within his father's logger jacket. They told me that Hayden was extremely independent and for some time had preferred to manage his hospital treatments on his own. However, he wasn't managing any more and I surmised that they must be dreadfully concerned about his unaccountable weight loss, his having become "pale and miserable" over the past month, and his refusal to undergo any further treatments. Hayden's eyes were downcast but I noticed that, when I turned towards his parents, he would look up at me. After establishing the parents' concern and confusion, I turned quickly towards him, meeting his gaze for the first time, and said, "Do you think your parents can stand up to your strong feelings?" Hayden was caught off-guard and uttered a defensive "dunno". "Well, why don't you put them to the test? They look strong enough to me but you'll never know until you test them."

I turned to his parents: "Do you mind if Hayden tests you to see if you are strong enough to stand up to his worries?" Although uncertain as to the nature of the test, they wholeheartedly agreed to undergo it. It was agreed that his father would go first and that his test would last exactly 15 minutes; his mother would then join them for her test, which was also to last exactly 15 minutes.

The physician, Cynthia, and I, retired to another room, leaving father and son sitting across from each other with a box of tissues placed midway between them. After exactly 15 minutes, Cynthia joined Ray and Hayden. The physician and I knocked on the door when Cynthia's test was up and were welcomed back into the room. The floor was littered with tissues so I guessed things had worked out as I had hoped. Everyone had composed themselves; Hayden looked somewhat relieved and was laughing for the first time. Hayden, with some pride, assured me that his parents could stand up to his strong feelings.

I then asked Hayden to give me a measure of his worries, as opposed to his fun, by holding his hands apart to indicate the "bigness" of each. I carefully took measurements with a tape measure: 50cm of worry and 15cm of fun. The physician reiterated that this month's chemotherapy would be deferred. Instead, I invited them to return the next day to meet together again.

The next day the mood was lighter, but Hayden and his parents still didn't know what to expect. I met with Hayden alone first and told him that his physician had informed me of his bad dreams. He told me he dreamt that a group of doctors surrounded him and pointed their fingers accusingly at him, shouting, "That's the one!" They then stood aside for him to see a truck bearing down on him. He would then awake from this nightmare. He went on to tell me that, as a young boy, he had been

Experience, Contradiction, Narrative & Imagination

responsible for the supervision of his intellectually disabled uncle. They had been crossing a road together when the uncle walked in front of an oncoming truck. Hayden recalled: "He went to the hospital, but before he died he had drips in him. I just about beat up the truck driver. I didn't think!" I elicited Hayden's feelings of guilt and self-accusation but did not challenge them in any way. I merely accepted his construction of events.

I then asked his parents to join us and requested their permission for me to hypnotize Hayden. They sat by my side, looking on with keen anticipation. I guided us all into a trance by inviting Hayden to close his eyes and then asked him if he could see a TV set in his mind, and enquired: "Is it black and white or colour? Is it a big one or a small one?" To further confirm the trance behaviour for both Hayden and his parents, I had Hayden levitate his hand by proposing he imagined a balloon being linked to his wrist by a fine string. While his hand was levitated, I told the following story:

A long time ago and at another faraway place, I was doing the job I'm doing now. A man came to see me. He told me he couldn't eat anymore, and that he used to really like his grub. "Why not?" I asked. He told me that it was a long story. I told him I had plenty of time and he could tell me the whole story if he wished. He said he had to. He had no choice. It had been bothering him for a long time and he had had enough of it. He told me he was a truck driver and had killed a man accidentally. *And ever since then, he hadn't been able to eat properly. "How did it happen?" I asked. He told me that he had been driving along when a young boy crossed the road in front of him. Then a bee came from nowhere and stung him in the face. Then he temporarily lost control and ran over a man who had followed the boy. "Well", I said, "you can start eating again. It surely was not your fault. It was the bee's fault!" He replied: "I know that ... I know that! That's not what I'm worried about. I'm worried sick about the boy". I became confused and asked him why. He said: "He'll blame himself even though it was the bee's fault. He was only a boy and surely won't understand." Now I knew I was getting somewhere. I told him: "Look, I've been doing this job for nine years and I know what I'm talking about. I want you to know that no boy would believe such a crazy idea." He immediately brightened up and asked me if I was sure. "Sure I'm sure", I said. And you know, he went home that day, regained his appetite and started eating again. He let me know later that his life improved in many other ways, although to this day he doesn't like bees much. But I guess that is easy to understand.*

I continued with some "trance talk" and then asked Hayden what his favourite foods were. After some thought he said they were Kentucky Fried Chicken and pizzas. I then mockingly warned him that if he didn't start to eat I would get some drips from the hospital and give them to his parents. They were then to put pizza on one plate and some drips on another and he would have to choose between them. He said he would definitely choose pizzas over drips. I then said that his parents were to insist that he jump up and down on the drips, saying: "That isn't food. That's for the doctors and my getting better!" Before he was allowed to start on his pizza, he should throw the drips in the rubbish bin. He assured me that this would be no trouble for him. I said, "At the dinner table, there's only *one* thing you're going to have, that's food". I gradually reoriented Hayden, who immediately grasped above his head for the imaginary balloon, much to his parents' amusement. We agreed to meet a day before his next treatment in a month's time.

I began the next session by asking Hayden if I could reassess his fun versus worry ratio. Everything about him and his family told me the result would be a good one. It was 120cm of fun versus 1cm of worry. When I asked him how this had happened, he told me that finding out that his mother and father "could stand up to my worries" had helped him cut down on his worrying. "I tell them my worries. I had tested them. They can take a lot." Both Roy and Cynthia told me that they had been unaware of the nature of his concerns and felt they had now convinced him that he didn't have to be "so strong". They said there had been big changes since our last meeting. Hayden was talking a lot, looking happy, not hiding within his father's logger jacket, and eating well. In fact, he had gained 4 kilograms. Now his plate was always piled up and he did not share my concern that he would become overweight. His nightmares had stopped and had been replaced "by good dreams of just nothing". He no longer saw drips so his parents didn't have to play "our joke" on him. The colour had returned to his face and he was able to look at his hair growing back, whereas before he didn't dare to. Cynthia commented that Hayden was no longer frightened of his treatments. Two months later these changes had been sustained.

I later discovered that Hayden was one of the worst reactors to his chemotherapy that the pediatric oncology unit had ever met. He would vomit approximately five times in anticipation of his treatment, after which he would persist in dry retching. He required medication and often had to remain overnight in the hospital to be rehydrated. We joined forces once again over two sessions. Hayden was able to train himself to substitute movies in his mind for the nausea associated with chemotherapy. Hayden was never to vomit again and endured the remaining treatments with equanimity. Things were certainly looking good for Hayden. He also applied for my assistance in relation to problems controlling his temper in the classroom and stealing. He informed me that he used his "self-hypnosis" on the problems with great success and then extended its use to studying and improved his marks and concentration. However, he refused to do the same on the sports field, as he thought it would give him an unfair advantage over others.

A year later, it was discovered that Hayden had another site for his disease. His family decided against further treatment as his prognosis was so poor. Several years later his mother wrote the following:

Hayden learnt to cope with many emotions. Adjusting to changes in his appearance was one of his greatest hurdles, along with trying to accept the fact that many things he longed to do would never be. Hayden had a collection of many things that filled his room. This included the many hats he wore wherever he went. Although Hayden's life was short, he accomplished a lot more than many others who live a lot longer. He made us realize that life is too short to worry about petty things; we should live life to the fullest. Hayden feared sleep but not death. When he died in his father's arms, we no longer feared death either. The most precious memories of Hayden we hold in our hearts are those two last years. Hayden was loved and admired by many. Anyone who took the time to sit and listen to him learned so much. Being a very unselfish and special boy, Hayden had many friends with whom he shared his thoughts and ideas. The hardest task for those close to him was not being able to relieve his pain; we could only help him cope with it. The pain and torment Hayden endured no-one will ever know, but we can only assume. Hayden has left us with the gift of love, patience, how to endure suffering and understand each other. Through him, we learned the closeness and the importance of friends, neighbours and family. This closeness is a lifelong bond. Thank you, son.

CONCLUSION

These three stories have in common the experience of people devastated by guilt in relation to the demise of a loved person: a father, a newborn son, and a handicapped uncle. In each story, the person believed himself responsible and was moving inexorably towards his own personal tragedy. Grieving, either in anticipation or in the event of a loved one's death, was blocked. Once freed of their respective modes of self-punishment, all were able to take back control of their lives. The approach I took was highly individual but the results were identical - that is, the person's guilt and self-blame appeared to evaporate. Recently, I have been providing guilt-driven people with these same stories and they have had a similar effect on their lives. However, my more general purpose is to bring guilt/blame more fully into the grief/loss discourse, along with the creativity of deep play.

NOTES

1. Billy knew of Michael White because his ritual of inclusion had been referred to as "Michael Whiting" in his residential community, so he was very keen to learn what Michael White thought of his predicament when he learned that I was visiting Michael in Australia.

2. Most credit for this case goes to Billy's therapist, Tim, and the therapeutic team who worked with him with care and perseverance over many years.

3. This story was written with the collaboration of Martin and Sally Lyttleton, and I thank them for their counsel.

4. A complete report of this story, written in co-operation with Hayden's mother, Cynthia Barlow, his physician, Dr Louise Webster, his social worker, Lynn O'Flaherty, and Mike Murphy, has been published in Epston (1989, pp.29-44).

REFERENCES

Epston, D. 1989:
  Collected Papers. Adelaide; Dulwich Centre Publications.
White, M. 1989:
  Ritual of inclusion: An approach to extreme uncontrolled behaviour in young children and adolescents. In White, M., **Selected Papers** (pp.77-84). Adelaide; Dulwich Centre Publications.

CHAPTER IX

"I AM A BEAR":
Discovering discoveries

David Epston

Previously published in
Family Therapy Case Studies
1991, 6(1).

Therapists often worry that their ideas about clients generating their own new stories, and so their own solutions to problems, are beyond the realm of younger children. In this case, a six-year-old boy has been subject to "expert knowledge" from the medical profession, but has not been able to see himself as having control over his urinary frequency. Child-appropriate themes (dreams, fantasy, magic and stories) are used to externalize and personify the problem, and build a context within which the boy could discover the possibility of new strength. A taped "story" helps consolidate his new view of himself.

I was introduced to Bjorn, aged 7, by his mother, Uta. By chance I had very recently returned from Stockholm where I had been teaching and visiting friends and their two children, Emilie and Bjorn. Visiting the Stockholm zoo, I took delight in watching two native bears playing in water and noted that Bjorn meant bear. So, I must have looked confused or seemed not to hear as Uta repeated herself. "Bjorn" she said, "like in Bjorn Borg!"

I broke free of my memories of Stockholm and replied with some excitement: "Yes, yes ... I know. Matter of fact, I know what your name means. Do you?" Neither Uta nor Bjorn knew. I informed them that 'Bjorn means bear' and felt pleased to make this known to them. Bjorn seemed not to know what to make of this association so I asked him: "Are you bear-like?" He was still lost, but grinned.

We entered my office and Uta took over. She informed me that Bjorn had been referred by a paediatric specialist whom they attended in the first instance on account of a kidney infection. The major symptom of this had been urinary frequency. However, antibiotics had been prescribed and the infection was arrested.

Despite this both immediate and happy outcome, Bjorn felt the need to attend toilets more and more. They returned and were given the opinion that this would resolve itself in time and an appointment was made to review this in 3 months. Bjorn increasingly felt required to attend toilets, so much so, in fact, it was interfering with his schooling as he continually had to absent himself and he found it difficult to sleep at night due to his frequent ablutions. In fact, on the way to our meeting, they had had to call into three petrol stations for the selfsame purpose. The paediatrician advised the family to consult me.

Experience, Contradiction, Narrative & Imagination

Uta informed me that Bjorn feared that he would wet his pants and that that had become an overwhelming concern of his. I enquired whether she felt that this 'problem' had been investigated medically to her satisfaction. She assured me it had but she and Bjorn's father were of the opinion that this had now become 'a habit'. "Do you think this habit has started to have a life of its own?" She lamented that this was certainly the case. Their answers to my "relative influence questions" (White 1986) developed a compassion we all shared for the plight of this young boy. There seemed little in his life that had been spared by the problem's humiliating prospect of wetting his pants.

As chance would have it, Bjorn, in an aside, mentioned that the day before our meeting, he had gone from "morning tea to big play" without having to go to the toilet. I seized upon this with alacrity and requested permission to record our conversation because I suspected this could very well be "bad news" for his problem. This both dramatised what was to follow and positioned Bjorn as its protagonist.

DE: *Now Bjorn, you remember yesterday, the 31st day of October ... it could be a really important day in your life, couldn't it? ... because on that day, for some reason or other ... I don't know yet but we'll find out ... you/YOU did something really, really important. You won over your habit. Before you couldn't hold on to your peepee[1] but yesterday you got some strength, some bear-like strength inside of you to do this. And I asked you because I think it's very interesting how it was that you were able to be so strong all day yesterday. Your strength ... how long did it last?*

Bjorn: *It lasted between morning tea and big play.*

DE: *Between morning tea and big play.*

Bjorn: *Yes, between them.*

DE: *So on a day when you were feeling weak and your habit was strong, how many times would you have gone between morning tea and big play?*

Bjorn: *Maybe about two.*

My introduction positions me as commentator, as eye-witness to events that are about to unfold before me. Subjunctivizing is introduced by the suggestion of "it could be a really important day in your life, couldn't it?"

Jerome Bruner makes a case for what he refers to as 'subjunctivizing' as a means to contribute to the creation of new possibilities and new realities. I am aware that this term is somewhat awkward but I remain faithful to it in order to acknowledge my source:

I have tried to make the case that the function of literature as art is to open us to dilemmas, to the hypothetical, to the range of possible worlds that a text can refer to. I have used the term 'to subjunctivize', to render the world less fixed, less banal, more susceptible to recreation. Literature subjunctivizes, makes strange, renders the obvious less so, the unknowable less so as well, matters of value more open to reason and intuition. (1986, p.159)

Mystery and intrigue are brought about by the proposition that "on that day, for some reason or other ... I don't know yet but we'll find out ... you/YOU did something really, really important." The frame of enquiry into what 'knowledge' made going from "morning tea to big play" possible is set by the temporal distinction "before ... but yesterday ..." The putative solution is externalized by the allegation that "you got some strength ... some bear-like strength inside you", connecting it to bear-likeness and objectifying it so that it can be matched up to the externalized problem - the "habit/problem" so-called. Uta had already conveniently separated the problem from the medical discourse through which it had very appropriately been interpreted and 'treated'. This double externalization allows the problem and the solution/alternative knowledge of self to 'face' each other. Instead of the problem speaking of the identity of the person, the person is now positioned to speak of and to the problem. This permits alternative discursive practices, many of which I have come to associate with unconsidered possibilities and previously heard of discoveries.

DE: *Yesterday, the 31st day of October, was a pretty good day for you. And you were telling me that you felt pretty proud of yourself for winning and not losing. Are you curious ... do you know what curious means? Are you wondering how it was on Wednesday you were able to be so strong? Are you wondering? I know I am wondering. I am very curious. Are you very curious?*

Bjorn: *Yes.*

By expressing my curiosity and wonderment rather than employing conventional evaluative/assessment/classificatory formats, I indicate the potential location of 'knowledge' in the other's experience.

DE: *Can you think of anything you did differently that you don't really want to forget? ... Did you have a dream or anything that told you what to do? Did your teddy bear tell you something ... did it give you some special ideas? Did your mum or dad give you some special strength food? What*

made you so strong?
Bjorn: *I don't actually know what it was.*
DE: *Have you got any guesses?*
Bjorn: *It just came up.*

I start by an open-ended question that I don't necessarily expect to be replied to; my purpose is more a matter of orientation to the doing of difference. I then expect, as is the case here, to propose any number of possibilities for the young person to examine and consider. Often a young person will quickly associate with one of them or be encouraged either to generate or discover one of their own. When working with young children, we probably need quite an array of these at our disposal, and I zealously add any novel sources to my stock. My intended purpose in proposing dreams, magic, etc. is to recruit the young person's imagination into the world of children, a realm I hope they will allow me into. A reading of children's stories can equip you with your own collection which should indicate to young persons that you are willing to enter their life-world rather than their being required to explicate themselves according to the adult world.

DE: *Your strength just came up. Really! Can you think of any other times your strength just came up like that? ... Maybe not just to do with your habit but when you are running, cycling or playing ... or swimming when your strength just came up in a hurry like that ... and lasted for a fair while?*
Bjorn: *It does it sometimes at swimming ... sometimes.*
DE: *So sometimes at swimming you feel very strong.*
Bjorn: *I feel I've got power and can go a bit faster.*
DE: *Really! Is that right? When does that happen?*
Bjorn: *It sometimes happens at backstroke or lying on my back and kicking.*
DE: *And all of a sudden you don't feel tired ... you feel powerful?*
Bjorn: *It just comes up.*
DE: *Is it a good feeling?*
Bjorn: *Yep!*

This series of questions attempts to locate further examples of 'strength coming up' and, once again, I am careful to suggest some likely sites: running, cycling, playing or swimming. Bjorn acknowledges possessing at times the externalized power/strength, but relates it to himself in a random way ("It just comes up").

DE: *Do you think you are growing up? And do you think your power has*

"I am a Bear"
177

anything to do with that?
Bjorn: *Yep ... cause I've got bigger ...*
DE: *Taller and more muscle?*
Bjorn: *Taller.*
Uta: *He has grown 5 centimetres in the last few months. We just measured him.*
DE: *Do you think you will grow out of this problem ... this habit? Do you think your strength will take you away from it?*
Bjorn: *I don't really know if it is.*
DE: *Do you think you are growing up and getting stronger and, of course, your habit stays the same but you are getting stronger? ... Look where is this power coming from? I know you have a powerful name. Do you think your teddy bear is giving you power? Do you think he is starting to worry about you ... after all, that's what teddy bears are for - to look after kids? What do you think teddy bears are for?*
Bjorn: *Make you sleep.*
Uta: *Actually he has something else to give him strength ... a cow, Micky. She always travels along with us.*
DE: *A power cow ... I've never heard of those before.*
Bjorn: *When I cuddle her, it makes the power come.*
DE: *How long does it take?*
Bjorn: *Twelve minutes!*
DE: *Is that all?*
Bjorn: *The power comes out.*

The first questions potentially link 'power/strength' to the notion of growing up, an idea particularly appealing to young people. Also, given his age, it is very likely that either Bjorn or his mother will report favourably on his growing up. And I then go on to speculate as to the source of his power and I do so because I am alternatively using Teddy Bear/Teddy Bjorn. Much to my surprise, his primary cuddly toy is a cow. Bjorn discovers from his experience a means to "make the power come". By doing so, he purports to be the agent of the externalized 'power/strength/solution'.

DE: *How do you do that?*
Bjorn: *I think the power comes because it was fun playing with her ... giving them food and milk.*
DE: *So do you figure it has something to do with having a good time? Is that*

why you get power?

Bjorn: *I get power sometimes when I ride my bike ...*

DE: *I can understand that. So look you've got a lot of sources of your power. One, bike riding. Two, backstroke.*

Bjorn: *And lying on my back and kicking.*

DE: *Lying on your back and kicking strong. You've got a power cow. And you've got your power teddy bjorn. You've got a lot going for you, haven't you?*

Bjorn: *Yah!*

The sources of power are reiterated and summed up. They derive from his own experience and his relationships to his fantasy familiars.

DE: *Can I suggest something and you tell me if I am right or wrong? Maybe you didn't know until we got talking here today that you had all this power and for that reason, your habit was winning over you? You didn't know you had such power ... you didn't put it together? ... You had power here and here but didn't put it against your habit, right? You used your power for your cycling, for your getting to sleep at night, used your power for having a good time, for swimming fast and kicking hard. But you didn't know that you could use your power against your habit ... you didn't know that. What do you think?*

Bjorn: *Dunno.*

This series of questions theorizes about his habit's current success. The suggestion that 'not knowing' both the existence and extent of his powers is his weakness obviates the 'not knowing'. The not known becomes known.

DE: *Well, first of all, did you know you had so much power?*

Bjorn: *I didn't really know that I had it.*

DE: *Is it good to know that you are no such weakling? Is it good to know that you are powerful?*

Bjorn: *Yep!*

DE: *This is no surprise to me. You know why? Two reasons - first, because I knew what your name meant. Number two, you look rather powerful* (turning towards Uta) *He looks healthy and strong. You know how you can tell a sick looking person and they certainly don't look like him. Can I just feel your muscles?*

In 'knowing' that he has so much power, he is re-describing himself in terms of powerful attributes, rather than 'weakness'/'growing down'/

"I am a Bear"

'wetting your pants'.

I ceremonially invite him to remove his coat and flex his biceps. His parents are in the health-food business and not surprisingly he is a 'picture' of good health. Uta looks on with pleasure in Bjorn's self-delight[2] at impressing me with his physical strength which augments the sources of power he can draw upon. Uta provides another example and that is her pride in how high he can climb trees.

DE: *What do you think would happen if you gathered up all your power? ... you've got a lot of power and a lot of helpers. If you got it all together and put it against your habit, what do you think would happen? Who would win, your habit or you?*

Bjorn: *Me!*

DE: *Good! I think so too.* (to Uta) *If I understand your paediatrician, Bjorn has had something of a setback and lost some of his strength and more importantly his confidence ... no kid would want to wet their pants ...*

Uta: *That's his main concern actually, he's always saying he's afraid of wetting his pants. That's what actually bothers him. I really think he has enough power because all through these times, he's never wet his pants.*

DE: *I didn't know that. You're stronger than what you think you are? Do you think you are stronger than what you think you are? Do you think your problem is trying to trick you into thinking you are a bit of a weakling when in fact you are quite a strong and powerful person?*

Bjorn: *It tries to say that ...*

DE: *What does it say to you?*

Bjorn: *It just says ... it thinks that I'm a weakling but I'm not.*

DE: *Good. What if you talked back to it?*

Bjorn: *I try to do it.*

DE: *What do you say back?*

Bjorn: *I say ...*

DE: *I just wonder if we got together and worked out some power talk for you. Do you think this would really scare your habit? ... teach your habit a lesson? Would you like to teach your habit a lesson? Teach your habit that it doesn't really know how strong you are? You can't be tricked into thinking you are a weakling? What do you think about that? Would you like to do that?*

Bjorn: *I always say at night ...*

DE: *Yah, what do you say?*

Experience, Contradiction, Narrative & Imagination

Bjorn: *When I've gone to the toilet maybe 12, 11 or 10 times I say: 'That's the last time.' If I have to go again I'll say: 'No, that's the last time and that's it.'*

DE: *What do you think would happen if you tried that after 7 times? If you said: "Look, I'm sick of 11 times, I think I'll get powerful after 7? What do you think would happen? Do you think you could do it if you used your strength like you are using it?*

Bjorn: *I think I could have done it because I've done it one night. I had to go toilet ... one night then I held it. I held it the whole night until the next morning.*

DE: *You didn't?*

Bjorn: *It was only one night it happened.*

DE: *That was a good night to remember, wasn't it?*

Finding out some information about his fear of wetting his pants, along with the fact that he never has, allows me to enquire: "Do you think you are stronger than what you think you are?" followed by the personification of the problem as a trickster, tricking Bjorn "into thinking you are a bit of a weakling when in fact you are quite a strong and powerful person?" This provides two self-descriptions, one based on the mischief or malevolence of his problem, and the other more in accordance with his mother and myself. Such a question has the effect of deconstructing the 'truth' of his problem's version of himself. This leads Bjorn to recollect having talked back to his problem and having asserted an alternative version of himself, one consistent with this version that has been both resurrected and generated by this conversation. The question revising down his self-assertion from 11 times to 7 times is important for allowing action to be taken at will rather than being contingent.

DE: *Look, you sound ready. You are old enough, strong enough and smart enough to go against this habit. Do you think you are? We might come up with some ideas to help you. Do you want to wait until you are older?*

Bjorn: *I'll do it.*

DE: (to Uta) *Would you be pleased for him to do it?*

Uta: *Of course.*

DE: *I've got the impression from what you have been telling me that you have got all the power you need. But it's all over the place. It's not there when you need it. It's almost as if you've got a car and you know petrol gives cars power. And you have got petrol in this tin over here, and this tin* over here ... but the car still doesn't go. You've got lots of petrol but you just haven't put it into the tank. Do you know what I mean by petrol tank? I think we've got to get the power into you. Okay?? And then you can use it for whatever you want to use it for. You can use it to break this habit ... or you could also use it to swim faster or enjoy your life more. You ready for this?*

Bjorn: *Yep!*

With problems of this nature that require young people to take responsibility for the resolution of the problem, I often use 'readiness questions' (White 1986). In the above, I restate the 'double externalization': habit vs strength/power by way of a rather elaborate metaphorical description.

Bjorn consents to bring his power/strength to bear on his problem and I consent to the requirement on our part "to get the power into you". That is the contribution others can make. I suggested that Uta drop in at her neighbourhood library on the way home and get some books on bears as I observed that, despite Bjorn being bear-like, I didn't think he fully appreciated the parallels. She was only too happy to bring his bear-likeness to his attention. I, in turn, promised to make a cassette tape for him and forward it to him by post. For working with young people, I have substituted recorded tapes for letters as my medium of preference and necessity.

White and I have written at some length detailing 'letters as narrative':
Letters constitute a medium rather than a particular genre and as such can be employed for any number of purposes, several of which are demonstrated in this text. In a storied therapy, the letters are used primarily for the purpose of rendering lived experience into a narrative or 'story', one that makes sense according to the criteria of coherence and lifelikeness. Accordingly, they are at variance to a considerable degree to those conventions that prescribe both the rhetoric and stylistics of professional letter-writing. By 'professional' letters, I am referring to those communications between professionals about persons and their problems. Typically, the persons who are subjects of these letters are excluded from any access to this record, even though their futures may be shaped by it. In a storied therapy, the letters are a version of that co-constructed reality called therapy and become the shared property of all the parties to it.
(White & Epston 1989, pp.125-126)

Much to my dismay, I became very busy and wasn't able to find time to make a tape. About a week later, I rang Uta to see if it was necessary and, if so, to make amends. Uta was glad to hear from me as for four successive nights Bjorn slept through the night without requiring to go to the toilet. Since then, he had remitted and she urged me to send him a tape. I did so immediately and booked another appointment.

The following is a transcript copy of that taped "story":

Hello, Bjorn, David speaking ... I decided against sending you this tape right away because I guessed you might need it a little bit later ... and now is a very good time to start listening to this tape. It might be the very best time to listen to just before you go to bed ... when it is dark or coming on dark ... or if there was a time you felt you needed more strength.

Your problem has weakened your bladder and I am sorry about that ... but little did your bladder and little did your problem know that your name was Bjorn ... now it probably doesn't speak Swedish ... it's probably an English-speaking problem so it doesn't know yet but it will learn that your name means Bear. Now everyone knows that bears are very nice animals, but when they get angry they can be very strong and vicious. And when I met you recently I had a sense that you had a bear-like strength inside of you. And I wasn't surprised when you told me that on October 31st you had beaten your habit and proved to it how bear-like you were because you went from morning tea time to the big break time without having to go to the toilet. You kept your strength. Usually if your habit was strong and it had weakened you, you would have had to go to the toilet twice.

You told me you felt proud of yourself for winning and, when you told me that, I could see the pride all over your face. And then when I asked how was it that you got so strong all of a sudden, you said that your strength just came up in a hurry and lasted for a fair while. Now, Bjorn, that's not the only place or the only time your strength comes up. And there were some other places that it did. And you told me that when you are swimming, especially doing the backstroke or lying on your back and kicking, you said: "I feel I've got power and I can go a bit faster". And you said: "It just comes up! It just comes up!" Bjorn, do you think if you got angry you could make it come up? I don't know but it's possible if you are as bear-like as your name tells me. And I wondered if your power had anything to do with your growing up. And your mum said that you were getting taller and more muscley. And that you had grown 5cm since February. This made me wonder if in the very near

"I am a Bear"
183

future you're just going to grow away from your problem and grow out of it. You also told me that you felt powerful climbing trees. And isn't it interesting that bears are famous for their ability to climb trees?

You have a powerful name, a powerful mind, a powerful body, and just one bit of you has been a bit weakened by your illness. Also you have some power friends ... you told me that you had a teddy bear, a teddy bjorn. And when I asked if it would look after you, you said: "It makes me sleep. It makes me brave at night". You also have Micky, the power cow. And when you cuddle her it makes the power come. Riding your bike also makes you feel powerful. So when I started thinking about it, Bjorn, there were many sources of your power. Your name, your bear-like name ... your physical strength ... your growing up ... your ability to call up and call upon your power when you need it - swimming doing the backstroke or lying on your back kicking ... when you are cycling ... climbing trees. These are all your sources of power. And you didn't know you had so much power. And you didn't know you could use your power against your habit. Your habit had better watch out if you put your power against it. It is a weak habit ... a habit that usually affects young people and it couldn't stand up to either your growing up or putting your power against it. So Bjorn, all you have to do is call up your power instead of just letting it come. Now it just comes up when you need it. Do you think you need your strength and your power against your problem to weaken it and strengthen yourself?

You said it was good to know you were so powerful. But I knew it, Bjorn, your mum knew it, you have a powerful name, you look powerful, healthy and strong ... and when I felt your muscles they told me that inside of your body there was a lot of strength. There's just one little bit of you that has been weakened by your sickness. But you're no weakling. Bjorn, you could if you wanted to when you need to ... gather all your power together ... you've also got helpers in your Teddy-Bjorn, and your Teddy-Cow. And when I asked you who would win, your habit or you, it was pretty clear that your habit was a weak habit. And that you could win. But it has made you lose your muscle-tone and your confidence, and made you afraid of wetting your pants. But remember you never have wet your pants.

So, Bjorn, you are stronger than what you think you are. And your habit is trying to trick you into thinking you are a weakling. It is not so! Bjorn, this is not so! So, look, you are a powerful young person, your problem is weakening you and making your miserable, making you not sleep at night. It is time to get angry with it, Bjorn, to strengthen yourself and not just let your power come up, but call it up.

Bjorn, there is a secret formula for this and I'm going to tell you what it is. I'm going to tell you what it is. What you have to do, if you want to, if you want to weaken your habit and strengthen you, to say this when you need it, and only when you need it. So listen very, very carefully ... to what I'm going to say now.

Are you ready, Bjorn? Really, really listen. And say after me when you need to ... you don't need to say everything but just what you like of my words. These are magic power words. Very, very powerful. Ready?

"Problem, I am getting sick and tired of how you are making me think I have to go to the toilet all the time and making me believe I am going to wet my pants. Well, let me tell you, problem, I have **never** wet my pants and I **never** will. So I don't believe you **anymore**. Problem, my name is Bjorn. I am bear-like. Like a bear, I am a very nice and cuddly person but, when I get angry, **watch out!** I have more strength than you think. Until I met David, I just thought my power came up when I needed it, like when I am swimming backstroke, riding my bike or climbing trees. Now I know I can call it up when I want to ... when I am **angry**. **Problem, I need to teach you a lesson you will never forget.** I am going to make you **wait and wait** until you are sick of bothering me. I have all the power I need to do this. And if I feel weak, I have a teddy-bjorn and a teddy-cow to give me courage and strength. And I have strong parents. So, problem, **you've had it!** You thought I was a weakling, a little pussy cat - I AM A BEAR!"

(**Bold** type indicates vocal stressing)

I am now making it part of my regular practice to provide young persons with 'taped stories'. Doing so allows us as therapists to re-enter the world of children, a world many of us have forsaken. Tapes allow for direct access and can be employed by the young person at particularly strategic times, especially for those problems/habits that are most troublesome at night, like nightmares, night-rocking, asthma attacks related to morning dipping, night fears, bedwetting, etc. These tapes are constructed with reference to the narratives familiar to children. So, when I am ready, I approach my dictaphone, place it on the floor and sit cross-legged in front of it and merely tell a story.

I compose the 'story' in much the same way as I might write a 'letter of narrative' from my notes taken during the session. I read them over several times until a story-line emerges in my imagination. In Bjorn's story, my hope was to convert the randomness of his power/strength 'just coming up' to 'calling it up' at those times he either required or desired it. I devised the 'magic, power words' as my vehicle for this transition from chance to volition. I also added 'bladder retention training' but removed it from the frame of a 'programme', and located it into the narrative as a form of revenge. Such a frame is only possible in an externalizing discourse, in which the young person can relate to their problem in some way or other. It also makes it likely for this young person to bear the discomfort of making his problem "wait and wait until you are sick of bothering me". The notion of "trick" admits of another version, another 'reading' of Bjorn's experience of his bladder and the urgency he feels.

Uta cancelled the next appointment 3 weeks later. She concluded it wasn't necessary as the problem had vanished and she felt that attending the appointment would be a waste of time for me as well as for Bjorn. I contacted Uta by phone several times up until a recent 6-month follow-up. She observed that his only concern was his unwillingness to travel on trans-Pacific flights and that they didn't feel there was any cause for their concern right now. She happily gave permission for me to contribute the above to Family Therapy Case Studies.

SUMMARY

I have been exploring for some time now the capability of young people to produce their own knowledges in relation to their concerns. Accordingly, my task is to assist them to produce their knowledges and, moreover, to know their knowledgeableness. For those adults committed to the view that children's problems are best resolved by the transfer of adult 'expert' knowledge, the notion that young people can generate their own solutions often seems strange. I advance two propositions: (1) taking young people seriously is hard for adults who expect young people to take them seriously, and, (2) hypnotic phenomena are children's play.

With Bjorn, the alternative story contained both a re-presentation of the alternative knowledge to its inventor and suggestions of how this knowledge might be applied at his will. 'Readiness questions' had reassured me that he was willing.

I refer to this approach to young person's problems as 'discovering discoveries' and my step-by-step summary follows:

1. Grasp the problem-saturated story.
2. Externalize the problem.
3. Personify the problem.
4. Make a discovery of a 'unique outcome', a discovery which contradicts the person's or family's 'storying' of events in their lives.
5. Speculate as to how this 'unique outcome' might constitute a part solution to the problem.
6. Invite the person/family to acknowledge this part solution as an accomplishment.
7. Elaborate the particulars of the discovered solution practices and invite the person/family to endow these practices with some significance in relationship to the problem, their description/s of themself/ves or their relationships.
8. Invite the attribution of heroic or virtuous properties for discovering their inventions; with young people, I suggest the domains of magic, wizardry, 'mental karate', etc. (Epston 1989, pp.45-46)
9. Draw distinctions around their knowledge-based practices and those practices that have organized family members around the problem and contributed to them becoming problem-bound.
10. Promote the person/family from person/family-with-a-problem - or a problem-person - to a person/family-with-a-solution - or a solution-person, power-person, veteran of the problem, consultant to other victims of the problem, etc. (Epston & White 1990)

NOTES

1. "Peepee" was the word contributed by Bjorn's mother, Uta.

REFERENCES

Bruner, J. 1986:
   Actual Minds, Possible Worlds. Cambridge, MA; Harvard University Press.
Epston, D. 1989:
   Are you a candidate for mental karate training? In Epston, D., **Collected Papers**. Adelaide; Dulwich Centre Publications.

Epston, D. & White, M. 1990:
>Consulting your consultants: The documentation of alternative knowledges. **Dulwich Centre Newsletter**, No.4, pp.25-35.

Gustafson, J. (in press):
>**Self-Delight In a Harsh World**. New York; W.W.Norton.

White, M. 1986:
>Negative explanation, restraint & double description: A template for family therapy. **Family Process**, 25(2):169-184.

White, M. & Epston, D. 1989:
>**Literate Means to Therapeutic Ends**. Adelaide; Dulwich Centre Publications. Republished as **Narrative Means to Therapeutic Ends**. New York; W.W.Norton.

CHAPTER X

AN APPROACH TO CHILDHOOD STEALING WITH EVALUATION OF 45 CASES

Fred W. Seymour* & David Epston

Previously published in
Australian & New Zealand Journal of Family Therapy
1989, Vol.10, No.3.

(* Senior Lecturer in Clinical Psychology
University of Auckland
Private Bag, Auckland, New Zealand)

Childhood stealing is a distressing problem for families and may have wider community costs since childhood stealers often become adult criminals. This paper describes a therapeutic 'map' that emphasises direct engagement of the child, along with his/her family, in regrading the child from 'stealer' to 'honest person'. Analysis of therapy with 45 children revealed a high level of family engagement and initial behaviour change. Furthermore, a follow-up telephone call made 6-12 months after completion of therapy sessions revealed that 80% of the children had not been stealing at all or had substantially reduced rates of stealing.

INTRODUCTION

Despite stealing being a relatively common problem, there are surprisingly few studies of clinical procedures reported in the literature. This may be the result of conventional clinical practice tending to include stealing within the broader classifications of "antisocial behaviour", "conduct disorder", or "juvenile delinquency". There is also a difficulty with defining and measuring stealing behaviour because it is usually a low frequency behaviour and by its nature is secretive, thereby making it hard to detect. Yet parents do seek help with children with stealing problems and may not accept a broader label such as "juvenile delinquent". Furthermore, whether or not stealing is the sole problem behaviour presented at counselling, therapists need access to effective and specific interventions. This paper describes an approach to stealing that was developed at a family counselling agency at which we worked, and provides evaluation support for its efficacy.

Our concern to find an effective approach to stealing grew in the first instance from a high rate of referral to our agency for that problem. For example, in 1984 almost 5% of families seen had nominated stealing among the presenting problems. Indeed, the incidence of stealing, as discovered in community surveys, is surprisingly high. In a longitudinal study of 110 middle to upper class children, 10% of parents reported stealing to be a problem with their sons at age 8, although this fell to 4% by the age of 10 years (MacFarlane, Allen & Hozik 1962). In a larger survey of children on the Isle of Wight, 5.7% of parents were concerned about their sons' stealing at ages 10 to 13, and 2.6% expressed concern about their daughters (Rutter, Tizard & Whitmore 1970). Furthermore, in a six year follow-up study of a random sample of 5,472 New Zealand boys, 10.9% had appeared before the Children and Young Persons' Court by the age of 17 years, and 72.3% of appearances related to theft, burglary, or car conversion offences (Fergusson, Donnell & Slater 1975). Although none of these studies attempted to measure stealing directly - that would be difficult to do in any case - they reveal a significant level of parental and community concern about the problem, especially for boys.

Additional cause for concern arose from the correspondence between childhood stealing and later criminal activity. Mitchell and Rosa (1971) in a prospective longitudinal survey of over 3,000 school children in Buckinghamshire, U.K., found early parent and teacher reports of stealing (and to a lesser extent, of lying, wandering and destructiveness) had a significant correlation with later criminal convictions of males, measured over a 15 year period. Also, Moore, Chamberlain and Mukai (1979) examined court offending in a group of 60 adolescent boys who had been seen 2 to 9 years earlier at a particular agency in Oregon. Seventy-seven percent of the boys whose problem had been stealing later had court-recorded offences. This was significantly higher than for a group referred for problems of aggression in the home or those referred for normative comparisons. In both studies the authors conclude that parental reports of stealing events constitute a predictive measure of later criminal activity.

It is possible that parental reports have influence on later offending because the child has been labelled as a stealer or thief. However, identification of a problem is usually the first step to change. Thus the most useful response to a parent-labelled problem of stealing is effective treatment. Up until the late 1970s at least, such an effective response did not exist. Reid and Patterson (1976) in a review of treatment of children with "conduct disorders", which included stealing, found that such children or their families were seldom offered treatment. The typical response was either a punitive one through the courts, or residential "treatment" for the child divorced from his/her family. Of those children treated by traditional casework and psychodynamic therapies, few responded positively.

The psychodynamic approach to stealing, as reflected in the few reports that are available (Levy 1934; Medlicott 1968; Meeks 1979; Menaker 1939), considers stealing to be a symptom of an unsatisfactory parent-child relationship. The task of therapy is the replacement of the symbolic gratification of dependency needs, achieved through stealing, with the original requirement of a positive and loving relationship. This is effected through the establishment of an intensive positive bond to a parental substitute, that is, the therapist (see Meeks 1979). However, a therapist's belief that the cause of stealing lies in an unsatisfactory parent-child relationship and a therapist's practice of not working directly with the family are likely to leave parents feeling confused, blamed and disempowered. Furthermore, when this "stealing for love" theory entered parent manuals (e.g. Gold & Eisen 1969), parents were provoked into scrutiny of their behaviour in order to find signs of parental neglect and often produced bizarre attempted solutions. For example, we have seen a 16 year old young man whose thefts from the family were met by trips abroad. Another family would double the "thief's" money. The solution was more "parent-giving" in the face of the child's "taking".

Assumptions about aetiology of stealing by behaviourists are more straightforward. The stealing "habit" is assumed to be learned and maintained by the reinforcements of material profit, parental attention and peer prestige (Reid & Patterson 1976). Thus intervention is directed toward the goals of diminishing social reinforcement for stealing (or suspected stealing) and providing punishment for the stealing act itself. This of course is not easy, given the fact that stealing acts are low frequency and difficult to detect. Thus many of the reported behavioural interventions took place in controlled environments such as institutions (Wetzel 1966) and classrooms (Switzer, Deal & Barley 1977), or with mentally handicapped young people whose powers of deception are presumably weaker than peers with higher intelligence (Azrin & Wesolowski 1974). There are only a few studies that deal with children in home/community contexts (Stumphauzer 1976; Reid & Hendriks 1973; Reid & Patterson 1976; Henderson 1981, 1983).

A further problem in treating stealing, according to Patterson (1982), is client engagement in therapy. He observed from research conducted over a long period at the Oregon Social Learning Centre that parents of stealers were the most difficult to get in for treatment, seldom carried out their assignments and had a high drop-out rate. This led to the theory - supported by the considerable amount of data collected from his families - that early stealing may begin from the disruption or absence of parental monitoring of theft and other attacks on property. The child thus learns to lie about his/her activities. In the next step the child receives a greater amount of unsupervised street time than normal peers and during these wanderings encounters older and more experienced antisocial children. The parents, throughout all this, may appear to know little of their child's offending. Worse still, they may not care about criminal offending by their child - a possibility that is also suggested in the correlation found between children's antisocial behaviour and their father's criminality (McCord 1979; Robins 1966; Mednick & Christiansen 1977).

The procedures described in this paper were developed with families who voluntarily attended a treatment agency. However, a significant number were referred by social welfare or police following community detection of stealing. The problems of engagement and follow-through of treatment were considered in both the design of interventions and their evaluation. Accordingly, results described here were from 45 families seen consecutively at our agency in which stealing was among the presenting problems, and we are able to report on engagement in treatment from initial interview. The treatment procedures developed have some aspects in common with the behaviourists, particularly Patterson and Reid (see Patterson, Reid, Jones & Conger 1975; Reid & Patterson 1976). However, ideas from other family therapy schools were more central to the therapeutic procedures, particularly as they addressed the issues of client engagement and the regrading of a child from 'stealer' to an 'honest person'. Indeed, the therapeutic procedures described here may best be regarded as belonging to the model explicated in the writings of Michael White (e.g. White 1986a; see also Munro 1987) and David Epston (Epston 1984a; Epston & White 1989).

SETTING OF TREATMENT

The development and evaluation of the stealing treatment approach described here took place when the writers were both on the staff of the Leslie Centre. This is a child and family counselling agency situated in Auckland and serving a large metropolitan area. Clients are either self-referred or referred from related agencies. Work with families is brief, employing family therapy models of intervention. Staff have a variety of backgrounds and formal qualifications.

TREATMENT PROCEDURE

In describing a treatment procedure that was carried out with 45 families and by a range of therapists (that is, the writers and other staff at the Leslie Centre), it is acknowledged that the range of therapeutic activity is of necessity reduced to a deceptively straightforward procedure. Thus this description represents a 'map' for therapy with stealing rather than a complete description. Such could only be provided by reproduction of therapy transcripts. The elements of the approach as outlined below were contained in all 45 families treated, not by way of invariant prescription, but as themes, tasks and directives introduced according to each particular family's unique characteristics and the pace judged as correct for their therapy.

Understanding the Family's Understanding

The first step in treatment was to gain an understanding of the family's beliefs and concerns about the problem. This included in the first place why they were seeking help now. With some families stealing had been going on for years within the home, and although it may have been a source of frustration, outside help had been sought now because their child had been caught stealing away from home. The referral may then have been motivated by shame from public exposure or by police requirement. Where counselling was sought by families as they awaited prosecution, we avoided direct court involvement by making this explicit in our therapy contract and, where possible, delayed therapy until the court had dealt with their case. Thus engagement with clients was explicitly for the purpose of helping a child become 'honest', rather than for advocacy of some future possibility of 'honesty'.

The descriptive terms used by families were noted. Theft from the neighbour may be called "stealing", yet the same behaviour within the family was called "borrowing" or "taking things and not returning them". A very low frequency behaviour may then turn out to be a common occurrence when all actual stealing is described, not just at its extremes. The therapists, by way of contrast to most families, adopted more candid terms such as "stealing" and "robbing" in order to contradict the reluctance of parents to be precise and to attain distance from any excuse-making practices that provided the child with 'cover'.

Questions concerning what is taken and how it is disposed of will reveal pay-offs from material gain. For example, a child with a restricted diet may steal food, a socially unconfident child may steal money to 'buy' friendship at school, or a teenager may shoplift clothing to maintain a standard of dress in order to gain peer approval. There may be no obvious material gain, as with the child who steals and leaves objects around making detection easy, or even inviting it. Such a child may be receiving acceptance in a peer group from the 'mere' act of stealing itself, or the 'pay-off' may be the several hours of argument with parents who seek an honest admission of guilt.

Such a conversation often revealed the parents' depth of concern as well as their inadvertent participation in the problem. Frequently parents responded to such questioning by admission of self-blame as well as confusion and helplessness. This in turn led quite easily to a discussion of the beliefs parents had as to the reason the problems existed. While some parents blamed influences outside the family, such as "the school" or friends, most had a theory that reflected poorly on themselves. Such self-blaming beliefs seem to immobilise parents from taking effective action. Providing an alternative or contradictory explanation (at the appropriate time) was used in such cases to release parents from self-blame. For example, a single parent who believed her son's stealing was due to her marriage separation was presented with an alternative explanation derived from her own description of his stealing history, which proposed that stealing was a habit acquired when he was allowed to keep spare change he found lying around the house, as well as from the sudden change from relative affluence to sudden hardship.

Engagement and Creating the Context for Change

Although the child's participation was sought in the initial conversation, special care was taken to engage the child directly. This is in contrast to behavioural approaches which were often conducted with the parents alone (see Reid & Patterson 1976). In particular, the child was asked questions around how well s/he was able to resist the temptation to steal, and how s/he did this. Other members of the family were asked to provide additional information about instances of honesty or strength in the face of temptation. This questioning had the effect of producing a description of child competence or influence over his/her problem that stood in contrast to the previous description, usually given by parents, of the child being incompetent or criminal. Thus relative influence - the problem's influence over the child and family, and the child's influence over the problem - was mapped in the way described by Michael White (1986a). By 'externalizing' the problem of stealing, and by clearly setting out to obtain a 'double description' of the person and his/her relationship to the problem ('honesty' versus 'stealing'), questions asked of the young person were experienced as sympathetic rather than exhortative. Also, the child, family and therapist were now effectively joined against stealing or temptation's influence in the child's life. Thus their firm commitment to therapy was usually achieved. Children who steal are used to adults interrogating them about their behaviour and its motivation and have often learned a manner of response that is passive and avoidant.

Further engagement of the child and family was frequently achieved through plotting the likely course of the problem through time. Thus children were asked to predict how much they would be in control of their stealing in, for example, two years' time. Personal agency was emphasised by asking them whether they would choose a 'criminal career' or 'honesty career'. Other members were invited to consider how it would be for them in the case of either choice. The outcomes of such questioning are not only engagement, but more specifically the discovery of new information by the family and the establishment of a solution context for change (cf. White 1986a).

Defining "Stealing"

It is necessary to have a shared definition of the problem in order to introduce tasks or 'experiments' which the family will undertake to generate change. Stealing by its very nature is difficult to define in such a way that all will agree on its occurrence. "Yes you did" ... "No I didn't" arguments are an integral part of the problem. Thus we adopted the strategy of defining stealing as the child having something in his/her possession for which s/he could not account, or an accusation of stealing by any other informed person that the parents had reason to believe (e.g. shopkeeper, policeman), or the parents' clear and considered opinion that the child had taken something. Thus the common situation of parents having to prove guilt, usually by obtaining a confession, was removed, with the child now having to prove innocence. That is, the situation was one of 'guilty until proven innocent' rather than the reverse. Thus emphasis was taken off the actual behaviour itself and placed instead on parental suspicion.

This change from the usual definition of stealing had two striking effects. Firstly, parents no longer carried the burden of proof, and thus the long arguments typical of this situation were eliminated. Parents were no longer constrained from taking action without their child's confession. Secondly, the child's responsibility was now both to refrain from stealing and to remain above suspicion. This was put to the child in the positive frame that it represented for them a sure way not only to "defeat" his/her habit of stealing (or achieve his/her total influence over dishonesty), but it would also serve to regain a good reputation, to redeem themselves in others' eyes. Most children could cite examples of being unfairly accused in the past, and most agreed that the restoration of their "good reputation" had distinct advantages which they had not previously considered. Parents, even if previously aggrieved, were able to join in such a pursuit. Children were tutored in some detail in the ways they might remain above suspicion.

Responding to Stealing Incidents

Parents were advised to treat any actual incidents of stealing by first telling their child that, according to the new rules, s/he had "stolen". Their child was then given a short period of 5 or 10 minutes in which to prove his/her innocence. "Proof" was to be established not by argument, for parents were specifically advised against arguing. However, a child may be able to prove innocence, for example by having a parent talk to a friend who may confirm that he or she had given away the article found in the child's possession.

Any act of stealing would then receive the consequence of one hour of work around the home and return of, or payment in lieu of, the article taken. Recompense sometimes required additional paid work if the child had insufficient cash. Penalties were assigned and completed immediately. No distinction in consequences was made according to the nature of the stealing incident.

Regrading to an Honest Person with a Good Reputation

Parents, and other adults if relevant, were asked to provide "honesty tests". Money and/or articles of the type previously stolen by the child were left in places where the child would be the only one to see them and be tempted to steal. These tests were arranged each day, or less frequently, according to the individual case. However, the actual "test" details were not to be revealed. Resistance to temptation was rewarded later that day by the parent complimenting the child on his or her honesty. For young children additional rewards were often arranged, such as having a favourite story read to them or special time with a parent at bedtime. If a child failed the test, this was noted and the incident was treated as stealing, with consequences applied as for any other stealing.

Honesty tests had the effect of allowing parents to leave money around again, and thus provided an opportunity for re-establishing trust. More importantly from the child's point of view, an ordeal was prescribed through which success could be faithfully established and proclaimed. Typically, at the setting out of the honesty plan, members of the family, including the child who steals, should be asked to declare how long the period of no stealing should be before the child would be considered an "honest" person. An agreed date would be derived from this, usually 3 to 9 months hence, and a celebration would be planned to mark off his or her change of status. Such a procedure has the advantage of regrading the child in his or her relationship to the initial stealing problem, and relationships with the victims can be repaired (e.g. Barlow, Epston, Murphy, O'Flaherty & Webster 1987; Epston 1984b; Epston 1986; Kobak & Waters 1984). Further instances of stealing would be predicted however, and if/when they occurred the family would renegotiate - with or without the therapist's assistance - a new date for the declaration of trust and honesty.

TREATMENT EVALUATION

Client Details

A total of 45 children were seen at the Leslie Centre over a three year period with the problem of stealing listed among the presenting problems.

In two families there were two children stealing, thus the total number of families seen was 43. Details of the children and their families are shown in Table 1. Consistent with community surveys, males well outnumbered females. Eighty per cent of the sample was under 13 years, so the procedures described may be considered as particularly relevant to younger stealers. One third of the families were headed by one parent.

TABLE 1: Characteristics of 45 children and their families treated for stealing

Sex:	Male	69%	(31)	Female	31%	(14)
Race:	Caucasian	93%	(42)	Maori	7%	(3)
Age:	7-9 years	44%	(20)	10-12 years	36%	(16)
	13-15 years	20%	(9)			
Living with:	Both parents	49%	(22)	Single parent	16%	(7)
	Step parent	36%	(16)			
Presenting problems:	Stealing only	47%	(21)	+Oppositional behaviour	53%	(24)
Duration of stealing:	0-6 mths	29%	(13)	6 mths - 1yr	7%	(3)
	1-2 yrs	13%	(6)	2 yrs -	51%	(23)
Steals from:	Home only	29%	(13)	+Neighbourhd	71%	(32)
Objects stolen:	Money only	38%	(17)	+Objects	62%	(28)
Frequency of stealing:	Daily	9%	(4)	Weekly	33%	(15)
	Monthly	44%	(20)	Less Freq.	13%	(6)

For almost half the children, stealing was the sole presenting problem. For others, presenting problems typically included oppositional behaviours such as aggression and non-compliance with family rules. For half the group, parents reported instances of detected stealing as having taken place for two years and longer. Many of these families had sought help now because stealing had begun to occur outside the home and/or their child had been apprehended by non-family members. Two-thirds of children were reported to have stolen from the neighbourhood as well as their home. In all cases money was taken, but over half had stolen articles of various kinds as well. Parents' detection of stealing was estimated as being daily for a small number, and for 42% detection occurred at least weekly. Given that detection of stealing seldom matches true occurrence, stealing was quite a high frequency behaviour for a lot of these children.

Treatment Outcome

Of the 43 families seen, only in one case was there failure to implement any intervention at all; that is, there was no engagement. In four further families, procedures were implemented initially but the family did not follow through. Therapist reports indicated then that the vast majority of families (84%) were successfully engaged in therapy. The 43 families were seen an average of 3.3 times. However, this does not reflect the full extent of therapy contact since a large proportion would have received follow-up therapeutic letters (see Epston & White 1989) and most received progress telephone calls.

Of the 39 children (from 38 families) for whom procedures were implemented and maintained, there were no further instances of detected stealing for 54% within a two month contact period, and for a further 40% only 1 to 3 instances occurred. Therapy continued beyond a two month period for six of the families, usually where issues in addition to stealing were problematic.

Standard follow-up procedures at the Leslie Centre included a telephone call made to a parent six months after the end of the two month initial treatment period, or six months after the last session if treatment extended beyond two months' duration. Thus follow-up reports varied from 8 months to over 12 months from initial interview. Follow-up also included the 5 families who had dropped out from treatment. Telephone calls were usually conducted by the primary case worker, who spoke to whichever parent answered the telephone. This was usually the mother. From the total of 43 families, 4 were unable to be traced at follow-up. Parents were asked a number of specific structured questions which allowed for analysis of whether stealing in the follow-up period had been absent, substantially reduced, the same as before treatment or worse. For the 42 children for whom such information was available, 26 (62%) had evidenced no stealing at all, and for 8 (19%) stealing was estimated as "substantially reduced". For 7 (17%) stealing had remained unchanged, and 1 child (2%) was estimated to be stealing more. In the case of 2 children, they and their families had been referred on to the Department of Social Welfare.

DISCUSSION

This paper describes a therapy map for families with a child who steals. Follow-up results are reported for 45 children (in 43 families) seen over a three year period at a child and family counselling agency. Results indicated a high level of engagement with families. This contradicts the findings of researchers at the Oregon Social Learning Center (Patterson 1982), who described families with stealing children as being particularly hard to engage. This outcome may be attributed to sampling bias arising from differences in the clinical populations. However, we believe that the better rate of engagement would follow from the therapeutic procedures we used, which place emphasis on direct engagement of the child and create an 'honesty' solution context in which all participate.

Parent reports at two months after initial interview indicated that detected stealing diminished or disappeared rapidly following intervention. At follow-up telephone calls made 6 to 12 months later, 81% of the 45 children were reported by parents not to have been stealing at all, or that stealing was "substantially reduced". This indicates a high success rate although the findings may be challenged on several counts. Firstly, it may be argued that the children had merely become cleverer thieves. This seems unlikely since parents who voluntarily seek help for a child's stealing are usually vigilant. Secondly, the reliance on parent recall of stealing for measurement purposes may be expected to produce some exaggeration of improvement, as may the fact the follow-ups were usually done by the family's particular therapist. However, in a single case design study involving four families, where the first author was the therapist, more sophisticated and detailed measurement procedures revealed similar strong positive results (Hamilton 1984). Furthermore, employing a parallel approach to our own, Pawsey (1988) has reported positive outcomes in his programme. Thirdly, the result may be challenged on account of the follow-up period being too short. Perhaps these children recommence stealing one or two years later? No doubt some do. Our procedures did not allow for long term follow-up of families. However, even if a number of children did recommence stealing, what this study shows is that their stealing can be modified - by their families and their own efforts - for a significant period. If it can be done once it can be done again.

It was noted in the description of clients that 80% of the group of children were under 13 years old, which suggests that the procedures developed may be more appropriate to a younger population. In this light, it is interesting to look at who the "failures" were. The eight children who apparently had been unaffected by therapy were from across the entire age range and were not over-representative of the teenager group. Four were under 10 years, two were 10 and 12 years old, and two were older than 13 years. Five had presenting problems in addition to stealing - in all cases oppositional behaviour. This is a little higher than for the main group. Another, more striking, difference is that all but one were male. The distribution of single or two parent households was representative of the larger group. Thus the approach is effective with children from all age groups, but there is the suggestion that children with a wider variety of oppositional behaviour problems, and males, may be more difficult to help.

It is our impression, gained from this and subsequent experience at Leslie Centre, that several obvious family patterns of stealing may contribute to difficulties in therapy. The first of these is where the child and parents are apparently emotionally distant and/or rejecting of one another. In such cases stealing is often characterised by the child's hoarding objects and/or making a poor attempt to hide the stolen goods from adults, thus appearing to invite negative attention. It may be this pattern that encouraged the psychoanalytic interpretation of stealing behaviour (Meeks 1979). Where this pattern exists, however, we would not adopt the psychoanalytic strategy of intensive therapist involvement with the child, but would work instead with the parent-child relationship directly. We have employed White's (1986b) "ritual of inclusion" with such children and their families, by employing the metaphor of "belonging". The child is considered as having problems "being belonged" and parents as experiencing difficulties in "belonging" the young person (e.g. Epston & Whitney 1988).

A pattern of stealing in which parental control is low is also difficult. The requirement that the child completes allocated tasks following a stealing episode requires parental ability to enforce this. This may be particularly difficult for some parents and therapists may need to assist parents in this area. This occurred for many of our sample of 45. With younger children, child management procedures as described in Seymour/Leslie Centre (1987) were employed. These procedures utilise some interventions derived from the behavioural tradition, but place them clearly within a family-systems context. With older children we often involve other members of the child's community such as peers, teachers, neighbours, other family members and so on where parental control procedures were inadequate. This was typically done through directly recruiting their assistance as monitors and coaches, or indirectly through having the young person write letters to them which would only be posted on the occasion of any stealing (Epston 1989).

Finally, where the problem is firmly entrenched in a pattern of stealing with peers, or older children, then the procedures described here are unlikely to work without considerable extension and therapeutic invention. A child in this pattern may be stealing as a means of entry to an antisocial peer group that places no value on honesty as defined here. Engaging the child around "honest" or "criminal" careers may not work, because for the child there is no real dilemma here. This is the later stage of the development of a child's stealing as described in Patterson's (1982) model. To be succesful with such children, therapy may need to proceed in tandem with the police, social welfare departments and the courts.

These difficulties in therapy with children who steal do not, however, negate the effectiveness of the procedures described in this paper. As noted already, children who were apparently unaffected by therapy in this sample of 45 children were a minority. Furthermore, when interventions were employed beyond the basic 'map' for therapy described in this paper, the stealing-specific interventions still performed a valuable part of the total therapy. It is our experience that parents will seek advice as to specific responses to stealing acts, as in the question "what do we *do* when s/he takes money?" This map for therapy provides specific advice, which we presume enables parents to depart from past feelings of hopelessness and frustration in respect of the stealing problem. It is also our experience that children, like their parents, enter therapy feeling hopeless and frustrated. By placing the advice for management of stealing incidents in a context of opportunity for the child to regain an 'honest' reputation, children, along with their parents, are offered a therapy of empowerment and dignity.

ACKNOWLEDGEMENTS

The authors thank former colleagues at the Leslie Centre, where this work was conducted, for their participation with therapy, follow-up evaluations and the ideas contained in this paper. We are also grateful for the editorial comments provided by Ann Epston and two anonymous reviewers.

REFERENCES

Azrin, N.H. & Wesolowski, M.D. 1974:
Theft reversal: An overcorrection procedure for eliminating stealing by retarded persons. **Journal of Applied Behavior Analysis**, 7:577-581.

Barlow, C., Epston, D., Murphy, M., O'Flaherty, L. & Webster, L. 1987:
In memory of Hatu (Hayden) Barlow (1973-1985). **Family Therapy Case Studies**, 2:19-37.

Epston, D. 1984a:
Guest address: Fourth Australian Family Therapy Conference. **Australian Journal of Family Therapy**, 5:11-16.

Epston, D. 1984b:
A story is a story. **Australian Journal of Family Therapy**, 5:146-150.

Epston, D. 1986:
Night watching: An approach to night fears. **Dulwich Centre Review**, pp.28-39.

Epston, D. 1989:
Temper tantrum parties: Saving face, losing face, or going off your face. **Dulwich Centre Newsletter**, Autumn, pp.12-26. (Reprinted in this volume.)

Epston, D. & Whitney, R. 1988:
The story of Dory the cat. **Australian & New Zealand Journal of Family Therapy**, 9:172-173.

Epston, D. & White, M. 1989:
Literate Means to Therapeutic Ends. Adelaide; Dulwich Centre Publications.

Fergusson, D.M., Donnell, A.A. & Slater, S.W. 1975:
The Effects of Race and Socio-economic Status on Juvenile Offending Statistics. Wellington, New Zealand; Government Print.

Hamilton, M.G. 1984:
Evaluation of a treatment for stealing in young children. **Masters Thesis in Psychology**; Auckland University.

Henderson, J.Q. 1981:
Follow-up of stealing behavior in 27 youths after a variety of treatment programs. **Journal of Behavior Therapy and Experimental Psychiatry**, 14:331-337.

Kobak, R.R. & Waters, D.B. 1984:
Family therapy as a rite of passage: Play's the thing. **Family Process**, 23:89-100.

Levy, E. 1934:
Psychoanalytic treatment of a child with a stealing compulsion. **American Journal of Orthopsychiatry**, 4:1-23.

MacFarlane, J.W., Allen, L. & Honzik, M. 1962:
A Developmental Study of Behavior Problems of Normal Children Between 21 Months and 14 Years. Berkeley; University of California Press.

McCord, J. 1979:
Some child-rearing antecedents of criminal behaviour in adult men. **Journal of Personality & Social Psychology**, 37:1477-1486.

Medlicott, R.W. 1968:
Fifty thieves. **The New Zealand Medical Journal**, 67:183-188.

Mednick, S.A. & Christiansen, K.O. 1977:
Biosocial Bases of Criminal Behavior. New York; Gardner Press.

Meeks, J.E. 1979:
Behavioral and antisocial disorders. In Noshpitz, J. (Ed), **Basic Handbook of child Psychiatry**. New York; Basic Books.

Menaker, E. 1939:
A contribution to the study of the neurotic stealing symptom. **American Journal of Orthopsychiatry**, 9:368-377.

Mitchell, S. & Rosa, P. 1981:
Boyhood behaviour problems as precursors of criminality: A fifteen-year follow-up study. **Journal of Child Psychology & Psychiatry**, 22:19-33.

Moore, D.R., Chamberlain, P. & Mukai, L.H. 1979:
Children at risk for delinquency: A follow-up comparison of aggressive children and children who steal. **Journal of Abnormal Psychology**, 7:345-355.

Munro, C. 1987:
White and the cybernetic therapies: News of difference. **Australian & New Zealand Journal of Family Therapy**, 8:183-192.

Patterson, G.R. 1982:
A Social Learning Approach to Family Intervention: Coersive family process. Castalia; Eugene, Oregon.

Patterson, G.R., Reid, J.B., Jones, R.R. & Conger, R.E. 1975:
A Social Learning Approach to Family Intervention: Vol.1. Families with aggressive children. Eugene, Oregon; Castalia.

Pawsey, R. 1988:
A family therapy treatment for pre-adolescent stealing. Presented at the **24th International Congress of Psychology**, Sydney.

Reid, J.B. & Hendriks, A.F.C.J. 1973:
A preliminary analysis of the effectiveness of direct home intervention for treatment of pre-delinquent boys who steal. In Hamerlynck, L.A., Handy, L.C. & Mash, E.J. (Eds), **Behavior Change: Methodology, concepts and practice**. Campaign, Illinois; Research Press.

Reid, J.B. & Patterson, G.R. 1976:
The modification of aggression and stealing behavior in the home setting. In Ribes-Inesta, E. & Bandura, A. (Eds), **Analysis of Delinquency and Aggression**. Hillsdale, N.J.; Lawrence Erlbaum.

Robins, L.N. 1966:
Deviant Children Grown Up: A sociological and psychiatric study of sociopathic personality. Baltimore; Williams & Wilkins.

Rutter, M., Tizard, J. & Whitmore, R. 1970:
Education, Health & Behavior. New York; Wiley.

Seymour, F.S./Leslie Centre, 1987:
Good Behaviour: A guide for parents of young children. Wellington, New Zealand; Government Print.

Stumphauzer, J.S. 1976:
Elimination of stealing by self-reinforcement of alternative behaviour and family contracting. **Journal of Behavior Therapy & Experimental Psychiatry**, 7:265-268.

Switzer, E.B., Deal, R.E. & Bailey, J.S. 1977:
The reduction of stealing in second graders using a group contingency. **Journal of Applied Behavior Analysis**, 10:267-272.

Wetzel, R. 1966:
Use of behavioural techniques in a case of compulsive stealing. **Journal of Consulting Psychology**, 30:367-374.

White, M. 1986a:
Negative explanation, restraint & double description: A template for family therapy. **Family Process**, 25:169-184.

White, M. 1986b:
Ritual of inclusion: An approach to extreme uncontrolled behaviour in children and adolescents. **Dulwich Centre Review**, pp.20-27. Adelaide; Dulwich Centre Publications.